Rediscovered for a Digital Age.

Edited by Samuel Gray

An Anthology of Tweets for the War Poets Association posted during Lockdown 2020 - 2021

ISBN 978-1-3999-2680-5

Printed in the United Kingdom
by Quantum Print Management Ltd

CONTENTS / INDEX

Patriotism & Sacrifice : God & Death /continued

INTRODUCTION

I am grateful to the WPA for offering me the opportunity to commemorate the brave soldiers who managed to compose poems expressing their thoughts and feelings and giving eye-witness accounts of the front-line warfare. A few poems were written in retrospect, but the majority are taken from letters sent home to families from the trenches, only published later. I am grateful and indebted to the recent research by Constance Ruzich, and her invaluable blog "behindtheirlines.blogspot.com". I must also express my gratitude to my benefactor George Worthington, of Florida USA, for his encouragement and very generous sponsorship of this volume.

I started in April 2020, tweeting Wilfred Owen's war poems, verse by verse, but I am not reprinting these as they all featured in my 1917-18 "Reciting Wilfred Owen" booklet, available upon request. However "Forgotten Heroes" starts with a one of Wilfred's sonnets, from his idyllic final summer of peace, in 1914, as a contrast to the other entries in the book.

The rest of 2020 saw an extended review of Ivor Gurney's war poetry, followed by women poets of WWI. In 2021 I presented poems by relatively unknown amateurs, whose surviving works are few, including English versions of poems by soldiers of several foreign countries, from both sides in the war, some of which may have lost something in the translation. The poems are not printed here in the order in which they were tweeted but arranged in eleven themes. These 294 poems, by 133 poets, have all appeared on the War Poets Association twitter pages.

Samuel W Gray

Occasional departures from this plan were made for specific anniversaries, as with our first entry:

7 April 2020 The WOA & WPA send warm Birthday greetings
to William Wordsworth, 250 years old today.

The Prelude 1799, lines 1-6, William Wordsworth:

"Was it for this
That one, the fairest of all rivers, loved
To blend his murmurs with my nurse's song,
And from his alder shades and rocky falls,
And from his fords and shallows, sent a voice
That flowed along my dreams?"

Futility 1918, lines 12-14, Wilfred Owen:

"*Was it for this* the clay grew tall?
- O what made fatuous sunbeams toil
To break earth's sleep at all?"

Wilfred, in 'To Poesy', his first poem in print, aged 16, dreams of being an original artist, refusing to "earn his pelf, slaving for the money-sack with the cringing herd":

"To be a *meteor*, fast, eccentric, lone,
Lawless; in passage through all spheres,
Warning the earth of wider ways unknown
And rousing men with heavenly fears..."

Wilfred's poetic response to the war was one of his trade-mark sonnets, peppered with classical references, but more aware than Rupert Brooke of the looming disasters for European culture:

"1914"

War broke: and now the Winter of the world
With perishing great darkness closes in.
The foul tornado, centred at Berlin,
Is over all the width of Europe whirled,
Rending the sails of progress. Rent or furled
Are all Art's ensigns . Verse wails. Now begin
Famines of thought and feeling. Love's wine's thin.
The grain of human Autumn rots, down-hurled.

For after Spring had bloomed in early Greece,
And Summer blazed her glory out with Rome,
An Autumn softly fell, a harvest home,
A slow grand age, and rich with all increase.
But now, for us, wild Winter, and the need
Of sowings for new Spring, and blood for seed.

ANTICIPATION & PREPARATION

Excerpts from Ivor Gurney's "Severn & Somme", nearly all of which were composed when in the trenches in Belgium and France, 1916-17. Most were sent to Marion Scott, who saved them for posterity. The first one is patriotic, written 3 August 1915, nearly a year before he went to France, in the style of Rupert Brooke, of whom Ivor was soon to disapprove:

"To The Poet Before Battle"

Now, youth, the hour of thy dread passion comes:
Thy lovely things must all be laid away;
And thou, as others, must face the riven day
Unstirred by rattle of the rolling drums,
Or bugles' strident cry. When mere noise numbs
The sense of being, the fear-sick soul doth sway,
Remember thy great craft's honour, that they may say
Nothing in shame of poets. ... Then the crumbs
Of praise the little versemen joyed to take
Shall be forgotten: then they must know we are,
For all our skill in words, ... equal in might
And strong of mettle as those we honoured; make
The name of poet terrible in just war,
And like a crown of honour upon the fight.

Ivor Gurney

"Strange Service"

Little did I dream, England, that you bore me
Under the Cotswold hills beside the water meadows,
To do you dreadful service, here, beyond your borders
And your enfolding seas.

I was dreamer ever, and bound to your dear service,
Meditating deep, I thought on your secret beauty,
As through a child's face one may see the clear spirit
Miraculously shining.

Your hills not only hills, but friends of mine and kindly,
Your tiny knolls and orchards hidden beside the river
Muddy and strongly-flowing, with shy and tender streamlets
Safe in its bosom.

Now these are memories only, and your skies and rushy sky-pools
Fragile mirrors easily broken by moving airs ...
In my deep heart for ever goes your daily being,
And uses consecrate.

Think on me too, O Mother, who wrest my soul to serve you
In strange and fearful ways beyond your encircling waters;
None but you can know my heart, its tears and sacrifice;
None, but you, repay.

Ivor Gurney, 27 July 1916

Ivor's "First Time In" the trenches made such an impression that he at once wrote about it to four separate friends, by the same post:

7 June 1916 (Laventie)

1. Dear Miss Scott,
... Here am I in a signal dugout with some of the nicest, and most handsome young men I ever met...
they sing their own folk songs with sweet natural voices... These few days with my Cymric friends are of the happiest for years.

Yours Ivor Gurney

2. My Dear Chapmen *(the Chapman family)*
...The faces and comradeship of the Welsh Regiment we are now with were worth going far to meet, Picture my joy.

3. Also the same to Mrs Voynich

4. and to Catherine Abercrombie:
... Thin faced and bright eyed their faces showed beautifully against the soft glow of the candle light, and their musical voices delightful...

Also, a week later, to Herbert Howells - 14 June 1916

My Dear Howells,
...Our first night in trenches was one of the most surprising things that can ever happen to me... Cridlan and I crawled into a signallers dugout, and so made the acquaintance of 4 of the nicest people that you ever could meet — and educated. They were absolutely first rate chaps. Unlike some men out here, they didn't try to frighten us with horrible details, but gave us as much help as possible... in making us feel at home.
Remember me to everyone,

Yours ever, I.B.G.

Three years later Ivor distilled his happy memories thus:

"First Time In"

After the dread tales and red yarns of the Line
Anything might have come to us; but the divine
Afterglow brought us up to a Welsh colony
Hiding in sandbag ditches, whispering consolatory
Soft foreign things.Then we were taken in
To low huts candle-lit, shaded close by slitten
Oilsheets, and there the boys gave us quiet welcome,
So that we looked out as from the edge of home,
Sang us Welsh things, and changed all former notions
To human hopeful things. And the next day's guns
Nor any line-pangs ever quite could blot out
That strangely beautiful entry to war's rout;
Candles they gave us, precious and shared over-rations -
Ulysses found little more in his wanderings without doubt.
'David of the White Rock', the 'Slumber Song' so soft, and that
Beautiful tune to which roguish words by Welsh pit boys
Are sung - but never more beautiful than there under the
guns' noise.

Ivor Gurney, 1919

"To England - A Note"

Ivor's first poem from the trenches

I watched the boys of England where they went
Through mud and water to do appointed things.
See one a stake, and one wire-netting brings,
And one comes slowly under a burden bent
Of ammunition. Though the strength be spent
They "carry on" under the shadowing wings
Of Death the ever-present. And hark, one sings
Although no joy from the grey skies be lent.
Are these the heroes—these? have kept from you
The power of primal savagery so long?
Shall break the devil's legions? These they are
Who do in silence what they might boast to do;
In the height of battle tell the world in song
How they do hate and fear the face of War.

I.G. 29 June 1916, Laventie

"Maisemore"

O when we swung through Maisemore,
 The Maisemore people cheered,
And women ran from farmyards,
 And men from ricks, afeared

To lose the sight of soldiers
 Who would, 'fore Christmas Day,
Blow Kaiser William's Army
 Like mist of breath away!

The war it was but young then!
 And we were young, unknowing
The path we were to tread,
 The way the path was going.

And not a man of all of us,
 Marching across the bridge,
Had thought how Home would linger
 In our hearts, as Maisemore Ridge.

When the darkness downward hovers
 Making trees like German shadows,
How our souls fly homing, homing
 Times and times to Maisemore meadows,

By Aubers ridge that Maisemore men
 Have died in vain to hold....
The burning thought but once desires
 Maisemore in morning gold!

O when we marched through Maisemore
 Past many a creaking cart,
We little thought we had in us
 Love so hot at heart.

I.G. 8 November 1916

Helen Parry was educated at Roedean and Kings College Art School, and became a poet.

"A Volunteer" - by Helen Parry Eden

He had no heart for war, its ways and means,
Its train of machinations and machines,
Its murky provenance, its flagrant ends;

His soul, unpledged for his own dividends,
He had not ventured for a nation's spoils.
So had he sighed for England and her toils
Of greed, was't like his pulse would beat less blithe
To see the Teuton shells on Rotherhithe
And Mayfair – so each body had 'scaped its niche,
The wretched poor, the still more wretched rich?
Why had he sought the struggle and its pain?
Lest little girls with linked hands in the lane
Should look "You did not shield us!" as they wended
Across his window when the war ended.

"Before Action" - by W N Hodgson

By all the glories of the day
  And the cool evening's benison,
By that last sunset touch that lay
  Upon the hills when day was done,
By beauty lavishly outpoured
  And blessings carelessly received,
By all the days that I have lived
  Make me a soldier, Lord.

By all of all man's hopes and fears
  And all the wonders poets sing,
The laughter of unclouded years,
  And every sad and lovely thing;
By the romantic ages stored
  With high endeavour that was his,
By all his mad catastrophes
  Make me a man, O Lord.

I, that on my familiar hill
  Saw with uncomprehending eyes
A hundred of Thy sunsets spill
  Their fresh and sanguine sacrifice,
Ere the sun swings his noonday sword
  Must say good-bye to all of this; -
By all delights that I shall miss,
  Help me to die, O Lord.

W N Hodgson, 30 June 1916

Alas, his prophecy was correct: K.I.A. a day later, 1 July 1916 at Mametz, - First day of 'The Somme' - buried in the famous Mansel Trench, inscribed: "The Devonshires held this trench. The Devonshires hold it still."

The Grenfell brothers, Julian and Billy, both went to Eton and Balliol. After Oxford, Julian Grenfell became a professional soldier, served in India and South Africa and went to Belgium in 1914 for the first Battle of Ypres, winning the DSO in November. 29 April 1915, Julian wrote "Into Battle", and died a month later.

"Into Battle"

The naked earth is warm with Spring,
And with green grass and bursting trees
Leans to the sun's gaze glorying,
And quivers in the sunny breeze;
And Life is Colour and Warmth and Light,
And a striving evermore for these;
And he is dead who will not fight;
And who dies fighting has increase.

The fighting man shall from the sun
Take warmth, and life from the glowing earth;
Speed with the light-foot winds to run,
And with the trees to newer birth;
And find, when fighting shall be done,
Great rest, and fullness after dearth.

All the bright company of Heaven
Hold him in their high comradeship,
The Dog star, and the Sisters Seven,
Orion's belt and sworded hip.

The woodland trees that stand together,
They stand to him each one a friend;
They gently speak in the windy weather;
They guide to valley and ridges' end.
The kestrel hovering by day,
And the little owls that call by night,
Bid him be swift and keen as they,
As keen of ear, as swift of sight.

The blackbird sings to him: 'Brother, brother,
If this be the last song you shall sing,
Sing well, for you may not sing another;
Brother, sing'.

In dreary, doubtful, waiting hours,
Before the brazen frenzy starts,
The horses show him nobler powers;
O patient eyes, courageous hearts!

And when the burning moment breaks,
And all things else are out of mind,
And only Joy of Battle takes
Him by the throat, and makes him blind.
Through joy and blindness he shall know,
Not caring much to know, that still
Nor lead nor steel shall reach him, so
That it be not the Destined Will.

The thundering line of battle stands,
And in the air Death moans and sings;
But Day shall clasp him with strong hands,
And Night shall fold him in soft wings.

Julian Grenfell

Philip Bainbridge *(First in Classics, Cambridge, then teacher at Shrewsbury)*

Though nearly blind, he enlisted in Nov 1917; friend of Wilfred Owen in Scarborough, and of Scott Moncrieff; killed at Épehy Sept. 1918, leading a forlorn patrol across a sunken road. Bainbridge's title is a humorous dig at Rupert Brooke's sonnet.

"If I should die"

If I should die, be not concerned to know
  The manner of my ending, if I fell
Leading a forlorn charge against the foe,
  Strangled by gas, or shattered by a shell.
Nor seek to see me in this death-in-life
  Mid shirks and curses, oaths and blood and sweat,
Cold in the darkness, on the edge of strife,
  Bored and afraid, irresolute, and wet.
But if you think of me, remember one
  Who loved good dinners, curious parody,
Swimming, and lying naked in the sun,
  Latin hexameters, and heraldry,
Athenian subtleties of 'dys' and 'poiz',
  Beethoven, Botticelli, beer, and boys.

Rifleman N H Todd, ed. Felsted School & Keble, Oxford, friend of Coulson (p.111) taught 10 years at Sedbergh, then, in January 1916, considered enlisting. A verse from

"Sweet Aldbourne"

"There lies a trench in Flanders far away,
Where booming terror thunders night and day;
And duty calls that ever gallant band
To fight for freedom and the Motherland.
So if the call to go across the sea
To join those heroes fighting comes to me,
And if I too shall act the greater part
With faith unwavering and a steadfast heart,
Surely the times that we together passed
Shall bring a happy vision to the last,
A vision of a Church lit up by prayer..."

Todd's father had been a vicar in Suffolk. Three months after 'Sweet Aldbourne', April 1916, he enlisted and wrote this poem from Hazeley Down Camp, while training, overlooking Winchester, 1916:

"A Letter"

Dear Meg, now I'm a simple Tommy
I thought you'd like a letter from me,
Living a silent celibut
With twenty others in a hut.
My bed of wooden boards and trestles
And blankets thick with which one wrestles,
While the cold night wind through the door
Keeps time to the rats that scour the floor.
A sergeant stern with language rude
Who tells me that my drilling's crude,
And boots two inches thick, which they
Make me to clean three times a day.
But even here where bugles ring
The Southern lark goes up to sing;
And nobly stretch the long white downs
O'erlooking Hampshire's famous towns,
Where years ago through woods of fir
King Alfred rode to Winchester;
And here is haunted, holy ground
Where Arthur held his Table Round,
And Ethlebert and Athelstane
Drove back the foray of the Dane...

N H Todd, April 1916

Written while at Hazeley Down training camp near Winchester in August 1916, untitled:

Dear Geoff I wonder if you'd like to be
A soldier of King George, the same as me.
To live in Huts arranged in long straight rows,
Or if you'd rather, call them Bungalows.
Your bed, three boards, on which you rest at night,
Which you're required by order to keep white.
To rise at six — or usually much later
And wash, and dress, and shave at such a rate, a
Bedroom at the P.S.S. would hardly equal,
Then marching; about for hours as a sequel.

To listen to advice from N.C.O's
How to stick bayonets inside your foes,
And many other military jaws,
And all the mysteries of forming fours.
A change indeed from that old room I sat in
Trying to teach the elements of Latin,
And bringing boys, whose names I will not mention,
In army parlance " to strict attention."
I hope when I return, if e'er I do,
You'll know your Latin Grammar all right through!
And have no trouble, when I am a civvy,
In reading off at sight a page Livy.

Meanwhile I wander sometimes up and down,
Along the ridges circling, Winton Town
Finding the orchids bending to the breeze,
Or lying on the wild thyme at my ease,
Or hearing ill the Minster's giant pile,
The throb of glory thrilling up the aisle,
And Dreaming of the Princess Who, years past,
Built their memorials, and only asked
Those who came after just one prayer to say
For those who went into the eternal day
For ever, where the tracery of heaven
Lets in the light from all fine planets seven.
And so farewell much love, and may we meet,
Where the swift Rawthey splashes round the feet
Of laughing boys, and Winder's dear old crest
Catches the sunlight dying in the West.
And laden with the spoils, the P.S.S.
Return with shouting in the usual mess.

N H Todd

"Memories"

Now I am a Tommy, a soldier of the King,
I find my muse, my rhythmic muse, most disinclined to sing,
It doesn't foster poetry, this everlasting drill,
Nor can I write a single line when doubling up a hill.

If you've slept between rough blankets in an army "bungalow"
And hear each morn at 6 O'clock the beastly bugles blow
And get ticked off on parade for spots upon your belt,
You certainly enjoy some things the poets never felt.

I cannot well Imagine Old Homer forming fours,
Nor Vergil at his post all night Guarding, the O.S. stores,
Nor Tennyson or Swinburne writing a pretty trifle
Upon the various beauties of the new Service Rifle.

If Hood had cleaned a boiler out or spent three hours in scrubbing
Or Shakespeare had to do his boots with special army dubbing,
I know that they'd have found their muse exceedingly retiring
Horace had never made a name for verse at rapid firing!

There is no Inspiration in the peeling onion "stunt",
Nor can you feel poetic when "looking to your front"
A heavy pack, a dusty road, a burning summer sun
Suggest my course to Helicon is very nearly run.

But if at last the day will dawn, when I can wear a tie,
And in the dust of memory my jagged putties lie,
When I return to civil things and have a decent meal
Perhaps I shall be able to write down all the things I feel.

N H Todd - August 1916

Ferenc Békássy was a bi-lingual poet from Hungary. Educated, along with his 5 siblings, at Bedales School, he then read History at King's Cambridge, 1911-1914 where he was a friend of Maynard Keynes and Rupert Brooke.

When war broke out, Keynes helped Bekassy to return home; the latter enlisted in the Hungarian army, but was killed four days after he went to the Russian Front, 25 June 1915, leaving this poem, sadly prophetic:

"1914"

He went without fears, went gaily, since go he must,
And drilled and sweated and sang, and rode in the heat and dust
Of the summer; his fellows were round him, as eager as he,
While over the world the gloomy days of the war dragged heavily.

He fell without a murmur in the noise of battle, found rest
'Midst the roar of hooves on the grass, a bullet struck through his breast.
Perhaps he drowsily lay; for him alone it was still,
And the blood ran out of his body, it had taken so little to kill.

So many thousand lay round him, it would need a poet, maybe,
Or a woman, or one of his kindred, to remember that none were as he;
It would need the mother he followed, or the girl he went beside
When he walked the paths of summer in the flush of his gladness and pride.

To know that he was not a unit, a pawn whose place can be filled;
Not blood, but the beautiful years of his coming life have been spilled,
The days that should have followed, a house and a home, maybe,
For a thousand may love and marry and nest, but so shall not he.

When the fires are alight in the meadow, the stars in the sky,
And the young moon drives its cattle, the clouds graze silently,
When the cowherds answer each other and their horns sound loud and clear,
A thousand will hear them, but he, who alone understood, will not hear.

His pale poor body is weak, his heart is still, and a dream
His longing, his hope, his sadness. He dies, his full years seem
Drooping palely around, they pass with his breath
Softly, as dreams have an end - it is not a violent death.

My days and the world's pass dully, our times are ill;
For men with labour are born, and men, without wishing it, kill.
Shadow and sunshine, twist a crown of thorns for my head!
Mourn, O my sisters! singly, for a hundred thousand dead.

Ferenc Bekassy

Capt. Eric Wilkinson M.C., who had already been bayonetted and gassed at Ypres in 1915, was stationed opposite Thiepval, on the eve of the Battle of the Somme, 30 June 1916:

"To My People, Before The Great Offensive"

Dark with uncertainty of doubtful doom
The future looms across the path we tread;
Yet, undismayed we gaze athwart the gloom,
Prophetically tinged with hectic red.
The mutterings of conflict, sullen, deep,
Surge over homes where hopeless tears are shed,
And ravens their ill-omened vigils keep
O'er legions dead.

But louder, deeper, fiercer still shall be
The turmoil and the rush of furious feet,
The roar of war shall roll from sea to sea,
And on the sea, where fleet engages fleet.
The fortunate who can, unharmed, depart
From that last field where Right and Wrong shall meet.
If then, amidst some millions more, this heart
Should cease to beat,-

Mourn not for me too sadly; I have been,
For months of an exalted life, a King;
Peer for these months of those whose graves grow green
Where'er the borders of our empire fling
Their mighty arms. And if the crown is death,
Death while I'm fighting for my home and King
Thank God the son who drew from you his breath
To death should bring

A not entirely worthless sacrifice,
Because of those brief months when life meant more
Than selfish pleasures. Grudge not then the price,
But say, "Our country in the storm of war
Has found him fit to fight and die for her,"
And lift your heads in pride for evermore.
But when the leaves the evening breezes stir,
Close not the door.

For if there's any consciousness to follow
The deep, deep slumber that we know as Death,
If Death and Life are not all vain and hollow,
If Life is more than so much indrawn breath,

Then in the hush of twilight I shall come -
One with immortal Life, that knows not Death
But ever changes form - I shall come home;
Although beneath

A wooden cross the clay that once was I
Hath ta'en its ancient earthy form anew.
But listen to the wind that hurries by,
To all the Song of Life for tones you knew.
For in the voice of birds, the scent of flowers,
The evening silence and the falling dew,
Through every throbbing pulse of nature's powers
I'll speak to you.

Eric Wilkinson M.C

The first of five German Expressionists - Ernst Stadler

Tri-lingual, from Alsace, and Rhodes Scholar at Oxford, Ernst Stadler wrote the history of German Criticisms of Shakespeare. A true European, War presented Stadler with a huge dilemma. When war was announced, his group of Alsace poets stood to sing their national anthem: La Marseillaise!

However, Stadler enlisted with Germany, and went straight to the front. He won the Iron Cross early in October, then wrote in his last letter, 9 October 1914:

> "I find this bravado somewhat wanting, and would wish for myself another object in life other than to have a grenade blow me into little bits."

Three weeks later a British grenade did just that, at Zandvoorde during the First Battle of Ypres, 30 October 1914.

This is a translation of the second half of his Surrealist Expressionist poem:

"Der Aufbruch" - **"Setting Out"** by Ernst Stadler - 1913

"But then one morning through the misty air there rolled the echo of the bugle's ring.
Hard, sharp, whistling like a sword-thrust. As if suddenly on darkness lights had started shining.
As if, through the tented dawn, trumpet-jolts had roused the sleeping forces,
The waking soldiers leapt up and struck their tents and busily harnessed their horses.
I was locked into lines like splints that thrust into morning, with fire on helmet and stirrup,
Forward, with battle in my blood and in my eyes, and reins held up.
Perhaps in the evening, victory marches would play around my head.
Perhaps we all would lie somewhere, stretched out among the dead.
But before the reaching out and before the sinking,
Our eyes would see their fill of world and sun, and take it in, glowing and drinking."

Engelke joined up for the whole war, fought at Langemarck, the Somme and Verdun, won the Iron Cross, was wounded in 1917, but returned to the front.

"An Den Tod" - "To Death" by Gerrit Engelke

"I do not want to do my country the minor service of sacrificing my bones, but rather do my people the major service of increasing the intellectual worth of the German Empire. No people hates the other - it is the powerful speculators without a conscience who manage the war." G Engelke.

But spare me, Death;
I am still in the first flush of youth,
My life-work is still unaccomplished,
The future is still wrapped in a haze -
Therefore spare me, Death.

Sometime later, Death,
When my life has been lived, when it has burned away
Into my work - when the tired heart is waning,
When the world has nothing more to say to me,
Then carry me off, Death.

Badly wounded in a British attack, Engelke was rescued by them the next day but died, 13 October 1918, in a British field hospital.

Five poems by Alfred Lichtenstein, another Expressionist, an ironic satirist from Berlin, trained as a lawyer. At the end of his compulsory military service, 1913-14, he was sent straight to the Somme as war broke out, and died a month later from wounds received attacking Vermandovillers, 24 Sept 1914.

"Doch Kommt Ein Krieg" - "Suppose War Is Coming" 10 July 1914

Suppose war is coming. There's been peace for too long.
Then things will get serious. Trumpet calls
Will galvanise you. And nights will be ablaze.
You will freeze in your tent. You'll feel hot all over. You'll go hungry.
Drown. Be blown up. Bleed to death. Fields will rattle to death.
Church-towers will topple. Horizons will be in flames.
Winds will gust. Cities will come tumbling down.
The thunder of heavy guns will fill up the horizon.
From the hills all around smoke
Will rise and shells will explode overhead.

Alfred Lichtenstein

"Gebet Vor Der Schlacht" - "Prayer Before Battle"

The men are singing fervently, each for himself:
God, protect me from misfortune,
Father, Son, and Holy Ghost,
That no grenades hit me,
That those bastards, our enemies,
Don't catch me nor shoot me,
That I don't snuff it like a dog
For the dear Fatherland.
Look, I'd like to go on living,
Milk cows, bang girls
And beat up that blighter Sepp,
Getting drunk many more times
Until my blessed death.
Look, I pray well and willingly,
Seven rosaries a day,
If you, God, in your mercy
Will kill my friend Huber, or
Meier, and spare me.

But if the worst should come,
Don't let me be too badly wounded.
Send me a slight leg wound,
A small arm injury,
So that I may return as a hero
Who has a tale to tell.

Alfred Lichtenstein

"Return of the Village Lad"

When I was young the world was a little pond
Grandmother and red roof, the lowing
Of oxen and a bush made up of trees
And all around was the great green meadow.
Lovely it was, this dreaming-into-the-distance,
This being nothing at all but air and wind
And bird-call and fairytale book.
Far off the fabulous iron serpent whistled -

Alfred Lichtenstein

"Prophecy"

Soon there'll come - the signs are fair -
A death-storm from the distant north.
Stink of corpses everywhere
Mass assassins marching forth.

The clump of sky in dark eclipse
Storm-death lifts his clawpaws first.
All the scallywags collapse
Mimics split and virgins burst

With a crash a stable falls.
Insects vainly duck their heads.
Handsome homosexuals
Tumble rolling from their beds.

Walls in houses crack and bend.
Fishes rot in every burn.
All things reach a sticky end.
Buses, screeching, overturn.

Alfred Lichtenstein

"Leaving for the Front"

Before dying I must just make my poem.
Quiet, comrades, don't disturb me.

We are going off to war. Death is our bond.
Oh, if only my girl-friend would stop howling.

What do I matter? I'm happy to go.
My mother's crying. You need to be made of iron.

The sun is falling down on to the horizon.
Soon they'll be throwing me into a nice mass grave.
In the sky the good old sunset is glowing red.
In thirteen days maybe I'll be dead.

Alfred Lichtenstein

Alas, Lichtenstein's prophesy came true: he was killed as early as 24 September 1914, attacking Vermadovillers, on the Somme.

Jean-Pierre Calloc'h, (or Yann-Ber Kalloc'h in Breton), was a Breton separatist, who spoke, wrote and taught 'Breton', which the French Republic outlawed in schools. He volunteered at once in Aug 1914, attacking the enemy wielding a sailor's axe, until killed by a shell in 1917.

Verse 4 of 7 from "Veni, Sancte Spiritus", Paris, January 1915.

It is long since I slept. There is a voice, in the winter's night, calling to me, a strange voice;
A strong voice, and harsh, a voice accustomed to command:
such a voice rings agreeably in young men's ears;
(And it is no woman's voice, nor the siren voice that haunts the Celtic sea);
A voice that none can disobey: War howling at the frontiers.
I will obey. Soon I shall be with my brothers, a soldier following soldiers.
Soon I shall be among the slaughter ... What signs are on my brow?
New year, shall I see your end?
But it is of no account! Sooner, or later, when the hour to approach the Father strikes, I shall go with gladness. Jesus is the Comforter of our mothers.
Be blessed, new year, even if, among your three hundred and sixty-five days, there should be my last!
Be blessed! For more than one hundred years have passed over this land, knowing only the anger of God, but you shall witness His mercies.
You shall see banished beliefs returning, the wings of victory spread again, under the beating flag of France, and our country exalted for evermore;
You shall see my Brittany free at last, and her language held in honour as it was when her knights were alive to defend her.
New year, year of war! Be blessed even should you bring, wrapped in the folds of your cloak, alongside springtime for the world, death for me.
What is the death of one man or one hundred, the death of one hundred thousand men, if our country only lives, if the race still lives...
When I die, say the prayers and bury me like my fathers, my face set towards the enemy,
And ask nothing for me of my Redeemer, except the last place in His Paradise ..

Jean-Pierre Calloc'h

Heinrich Lersch joined up in August 1914 and published:
"Deutschland muss leben und wenn wir sterben müssen!"
= "Germany has to live, even if we have to die!"
also known by its first line as: "Lass mich geh'n Mutter, lass mich geh'n!"
= "Let me go, mother, let me go!"

[Having been buried alive in a trench by a shell explosion, Lersch was later invalided out of the army, mid-1915]

"Soldatenabschied" = Farewell to soldiers

Let me go, mother, let me go!
All that crying can't do us any more
because we're going to protect the fatherland!
Let me go, mother, let me go.
I want to kiss your last greeting from the mouth:
Germany has to live, even if we have to die!

We are free, father, we are free!
The hot life burns deep in the heart
We weren't free, we couldn't give it.
We are free, father, we are free!
You yourself once called in Kugelgussen:
Germany has to live, even if we have to die!

God calls us, my wife, God calls us!
Who created our home, bread and fatherland,
Justice and courage and love, these are his weapons,
God calls us, my wife, God calls us!
When we atone for our happiness with grief:
Germany has to live, even if we have to die!

Comfort yourself, dearest, comfort yourself!
Now I want to join the others
you shall not free a cowardly servant!
Comfort yourself, dearest, comfort yourself!
Like the first time we want to kiss:
Germany has to live, even if we have to die!

Well goodbye people, goodbye!
And when we fall for you and our future
should echo over to you as the last greeting:
Well goodbye, people, goodbye!
A free German doesn't have to be cold:
Germany has to live, even if we have to die!

1914

America's troops mostly crossed the Atlantic in 1918. These next two sonnets were both written by John Allen Wyeth, the first during that hot summer voyage, the next one in the Autumn. The mood of "lonely/loneliness" links them both, despite the comforts of ragtime and jazz.

"The Transport"

A thick still heat stifles the dim saloon.
The rotten air hangs heavy on us all,
and trails a steady penetrating steam
of hot wet flannel and the evening's mess.

Close bodies swaying, catcalls out of tune,
while the jazz band syncopates the Darktown Strutters Ball,
we crowd like minnows in a muddy stream.
O God, even here a sense of loneliness...

I grope my way on deck to watch the moon
gleam sharply where the shadows rise and fall
in the immense disturbance of the sea.
And like the vast possession of a dream
that black ship, and the pale sky's emptiness,
and this great wind become a part of me.

John Allan Wyeth

"Night Watch"

Autumn and dusk - a band far off plays "I -
ain't got nobo - dy and nobo - dy cares for me".
Already autumn here in this new part
of France - the garden has a bitter reek!
How lonely stars look in a changing sky -
I turn the lights on so as not to see.
Already late for my night watch to start.
Silence too strong for anything to creak.
The night is very wide - the room turns sly,
and things keep still to watch what there may be
back of my tight shut eyes and secret smile.
Are you there? - and like the heart of God my heart
is vast with love and pain and very bleak -
O France, be still in here a little while.

J. A. Wyeth

Two sonnets by Alec De Candole, fearing for a friend:
[The title means 'those who are setting out'.]

"Proficiscienti I"

NOW God be with you wheresoe'er you go;
God knows I would that I could go instead;
My little worthless life - dear friend, you know
How little loss it were if I were dead.
But you tune songs such as I fain would sing,
You have dared such things as would that I could do ;
In music, action, suffering, everything.
My sum is still a moiety of you.
Go, since you must, those strange and fearful ways.
Where death screams loud in hurtling of a shell;
Would I might too! - But though my body stays,
My spirit goes with you to the heart of hell.
For souls once stamped with love's immortal brand
Eternally inseparable stand.

"Proficiscienti II"

Full merrily you went; yet my heart yearned
That you should go from England once again,
To tread the paths of death and danger spurned,
The darkling troublous ways of fear and pain.
Happier I was myself to go away;
For then the man that went, perchance to die,
By life and death's grim borderland to stray,
Was not a friend of mine, but merely I.
Call me not fool or braggart, if I know
That love awaked, in ev'n so poor a heart
As mine, desires and pants and suffers so.
To serve what is of its own self a part;
Nor even death can sever loves so sweet;
If not on earth, beyond it, we shall meet.

Alec de Candole

ATTACK

John Arthur Gray, DCM.
Enlisted as regular soldier with Royal Berkshires in 1905, and served in India until moved to France, Autumn 1914. Badly wounded in head during the attack on Aubers Ridge, to capture Neuve Chapelle, March 1915. Promoted to Company Sergeant-Major. To Fromelles, where he won the DCM for conspicuous gallantry, 9 May 1915. The shrapnel in his brain still pained him, so back to England, but in November 1916 commissioned as a Lieutenant. To Bapaume, as Germans withdrew to Hindenberg Line in 1917, and killed in an attack, 4 March 1917.

"Neuve Chapelle"
- [verses 1 & 2, of 7, and end of verse 6]

Six months of misery, six months of hell,
Drenched an' 'arf frozen, but sticking it well;
Sniped in the darkness, an' shelled in the light,
Gawd! 'ow we longed for the chance of a fight.
Diggin all night wi' mud to our knees
Workin' like demons in case we should freeze.
Would the sun never shine? We were stuck in our trench
Wi' the mud, an' the rain! one continual drench
Was wot we 'ad to stick. An' we dreamed every day
Of our pals who 'ad gone, an' the debts we'd to pay.
Till at last came the order - "Go back fer a rest!"
We 'ad seven days o' that, an' I likes work the best,
If that's wot they calls restin' - a drilling all day,
An' diggin' all night - but 'twas making the way
For a glorious attack, so we done the work well.
Then the order came - "Boys, you've to take Neuve Chapelle."

Royal Berkshires an' Lincolns to lead the attack,
Irish Rifles an' Rifle Brigade at their back.
An' the Iron Dook 'imself never led troops more fine
Than the old 25th Brigade - "Pride 'o the Line!"
Well, we marched out o' billets all singin' an' gay,
At the thoughts of a beautiful scrap the next day.
Till the order came down - "No more singin' - no noise,
We are near the position; no more talkin', boys!"
Then in silence we marched to the trench, just an old
Bit o' ditch, full o' water, an' perishing cold.
An' that long weary wait fer the dawn to appear
Will stick in my memory fer many a year.
At last came the mornin', an' with it a strange
Sort o' silence - then boom! as the guns get the range.

"Fix bay'nets, stand steady, an' keep in line well;
An' get ready, boys, fer to take Neuve Chapelle."

.... But 'ark! such a cheer
Rends the air, an' we know they 'ave passed through that hell,
"An' the old 25th Brigade's took Neuve Chapelle!"
John Arthur Gray, DCM.

Although his sight was damaged by the gas at Ypres, Wilkinson returned to his battalion just in time for an attack on Passchendaele Ridge, 9 October 1917, in which he was killed.

"Twentieth-Century Civilisation"

There's a roar like a thousand hells set free,
And the riven, tortured ground
Sways like a tempest-smitten tree;
And the earth shoots up in jets all around
And blows like spray at sea
When the wild white horses chafe and fret
Till the boulders back on the beach are wet
With the far-flung foam. But the hollow sound
Of the waves that roar on the shifting shore
Would be lost and drowned in the furious din,
When these fruits of man's great brain begin
To pound the ditch that we are in.
The trench is soon a hideous mess
Of yawning holes and scattered mud
And tangled wire and splintered wood,
And some poor shapeless things you'd guess
Were once made up of nerve and blood,
But now are no more good
Than the tattered sandbags - nay, far less,
For these can still be used again.
(Heed not the dark-red stain,
For that will quickly disappear
In the sun and wind and rain).
Above our heads - not very high
As they fall on the German trenches near-
Our own shells hurtle wailing by
But the noise cannot deaden the dreadful cry
Of a soul torn out of the shattered form;

While those who are still survivors try
(Like a ship - any port in a storm)
To hide in the holes the shells have made

And blindly, grimly, wait
Till the storm of shot and shell abate,
And it's "Bayonets up!" and blade to blade,
We can strike for ourselves and the brave dead boys,
Who, hiding in holes, have met their fate
Like rats in a trap;
But we perhaps shall have better hap,
For already there's less of the awful noise,
We can hear the machine guns stuttering death.
They're coming at last! And we draw our breath
Through hard-clenched teeth, as our bullets fly
Towards the serried ranks that are drawing nigh;
They stagger and fall, but still press on
To the goal they think they have nearly won.
And we wait and wait till they're almost here,
Then it's "Up, lads! Up! Let 'em have the steel!"
With a wild hoarse yell that is half a cheer,
We are out and their torn ranks backwards reel.
Then back to the trench to bury and build,
And count our wounded and count our killed;
But out in the front there are many who lie,
Their dead eyes turned to the quiet sky -
We have given our own lads company.

Capt. Eric Wilkinson M C

Alan Seeger, an American volunteer, k.i.a. Belloy-en-Santerre, Somme, 4 July 1916.

"**The Aisne**" - by Alan Seeger

We saw the fire on the tragic slopes
Where the flood-tide of France's early gain,
Big with wrecked promise and abandoned hopes,
Broke in a surf of blood along the Aisne
The charge her heroes left us, we assumed,
What dying, they reconquered, we preserved,
In the chill trenches, harried, shelled, entombed,
Winter came down on us, but no man swerved.
Winter came down on us. The low clouds, torn
In the stark branches of the riven pines,
Blurred the white rockets that from dusk till morn
Traced the wide curve of the close-grappling lines.
Craonne, before thy cannon-swept plateau,
Where like sere leaves lay strewn September's dead,
I found for all things I forfeited
A recompense I would not now forgo.

For that high fellowship was ours then
With those who, championing another's good,
More than dull Peace or its poor votaries could,
Taught us the dignity of being men
There we drained deeper the deep cup of life,
And on sublimer summits came to learn,
After soft things, the terrible and stern,
After sweet Love, the majesty of Strife;
There where we faced under those frowning heights
The blast that maims, the hurricane that kills;
There where the watch-lights on the winter hills
Flickered like balefire through inclement nights;
There where, firm links in the unyielding chain,
Where fell the long-planned blow and fell in vain -
Hearts worthy of the honour and the trial,
We helped to hold the lines along the Aisne.

Alan Seeger 1915

A poem by Peter Baum, a German stretcher-bearer, killed in June 1916 by shrapnel, aged 46.

"Am Beginn des Krieges"

At the beginning of the war there was a rainbow.
Birds, black, wheeled against grey clouds.
Pigeons shone silver as on their circular journey
They turned through a narrow strip of sunlight.

Battle takes place hard by battle. They lied like troopers.
Row upon row of staved-in heads fill one with horror.
Shells often explode
As they tumble on beginning to lose velocity.
The shells' pain-bow grows all the time.

Caught between Death and the bow of peace,
They clutch their rifle barrels more firmly, to defend their homeland,
Spitting at the enemy, leaning on one another as they totter,
Tumbling over hills, like waves of the sea,
Staggering on, attracted magnetically by Death.

Peter Baum

Three poems about primitive aircraft, one, surprisingly, by Jessie Pope, better known for her recruiting jingles; the other by an officer in the Artillery who fought the first 2 Battles of Ypres, then trained in a BE2c plane as an Observer.

The 'Taube' was the first German reconnaissance plane.

"To a Taube"

Above the valley, rich and fair,
On flashing pinions, glittering, gay,
You hover in the upper air,
A bird of prey.

Snarling across the empty blue
You curve and skim, you dip and soar,
A dove in flight, and shape, and hue -
The dove of war.

Above the soldier and the slain,
An armoured bird, you hang on high,
Directed by a human brain,
A human eye.

A thirsty hunter out for blood -
Drinking adventure to the dregs -
Where hidden camps the country stud
You drop your eggs.

Thus, man who reasons and invents,
Has inconsistently designed
The conquest of the elements
To kill his kind.

by Jessie Pope

Having crashed while learning to fly, Alchin spent 5 months recovering, joined the RAF, surviving 2000 more hours in the air; later a Squadron Cdr. and decorated with the Air Force Cross.

"**A Song of the Air**" by Gordon Alchin

This is the song of the Man -
  The driving, striving man,
  The chosen, frozen man: -
The pilot, the man-at-the-wheel,
  Whose limit is all that he can,
  And beyond, if the need is real!
Hey ho! for the Man!

This is the song of the Gun -
  The muttering, stuttering gun,
  The maddening, gladdening gun: -
That chuckles with evil glee
  At the last, long dive of the Hun,
  With its end in eternity!
Hey ho! for the Gun!

This is the song of the Air -
  The lifting, drifting air,
  The eddying, steadying air,
The wine of its limitless space: -
  May it nerve us at last to dare
  Even death with undaunted face!
Hey ho! for the Air!

This is the song of the Plane -
  The creaking, shrieking plane,
  The throbbing, sobbing plane,
And the moaning, groaning wires: -
  The engine - missing again!
  One cylinder never fires!
Hey ho! for the Plane!

"The Air Raid" by Don White

Above in the still and starlit sky
Smiles the full moon serene;
When a sound we hear that all men fear -
The pulse of the bomb machine.

The Hun rides on his raid tonight,
Death runs wild and free;
And terror wakes and cold fear shakes
The hearts of the soldiery.

Silent, ghostly cottages
Huddle beneath the skies,
And the frantic glare of rockets there
Glows fitfully and dies.

Silent are the moonlit streets,
Men seek the shadows there;
The awful breath of winnowing death
Is pulsing through the air.

Great God! To feel the helplessness
And the shame of naked fear!
To sit and wait in impotent hate
As the hawk of Hell draws near.

Suddenly the whirring stops
And thin high whistles sound;
There's blinding flash, a final crash,
And then silence all around.

And a little man in blue lies low
Under the moon's pale light;
In a pool of red, he is lying dead,
In the silence of the night.

"Ypres Salient" by Claude Temple

Tempest of iron prepared the advance of a host 'gainst a remnant;
Tempest of shouting announced the advance of that host
overwhelming,
And as the black rocks o'erwhelmed but unvanquished make stand
'gainst the ocean,
So did that glorious remnant make stand 'gainst that host
overwhelming,
Till the war pride and war lust of that host like the rage of the ocean,
Broke and recoiled from the wall of their stubborn unyielding
resistance.
How many times, say, when you were a host strong and we were a
remnant,
When you had guns by the thousand and we had to make war
without them,
How many times did you come in your thousands to conquer that
salient,
Only to find there the spirit of Agincourt like a flame storm fanned
Burning unquenched in the hearts and the souls of that
unvanquished army.
Did you not know in the heart of your hearts when your orders were
issued,
When you advanced in the pride of your war lust and glittering harness,
Did ye not know that the men of that little contemptible army
Come of that race that are known as the stubbornest fighters the
world through?
Surely ye knew in the heart of your hearts when your orders were
issued,
When you were told to go right through to Ypres or to die in the failure,
That you were never the match of that little contemptible army?

The 'Old Contemptibles' was the nickname for the British Expeditionary Force, the small army of regulars which was rushed to France and Belgium in August 1914. Named after an insult by the Kaiser Wilhelm II: "General French's contemptible little army."

TRENCHES & NIGHT

W N Hodgson, 1st in Classics, Oxon. 1913, Devonshire Regiment, Won MC at Loos, 25 September 1915, (where Kipling's son went missing). After holding a captured German trench for 36 hours, he composed "Back to Rest" on the march back from Loos, 2 days later, 27 September 1915.

"Back To Rest"

A leaping wind from England,
The skies without a stain,
Clean cut against the morning
Slim poplars after rain,
The foolish noise of sparrows
And starlings in a wood -
After the grime of battle
We know that these are good.
Death whining down from Heaven,
Death roaring from the ground,
Death stinking in the nostril,
Death shrill in every sound,
Doubting we charged and conquered -
Hopeless we struck and stood.
Now when the fight is ended
We know that it was good.
We that have seen the strongest
Cry like a beaten child,
The sanest eyes unholy,
The cleanest hands defiled,
We that have known the heart blood
Less than the lees of wine,
We that have seen men broken,
We know man is divine.

W N Hodgson

Capt. Colwyn Erasmus Phillips, Royal Horse Guards. K.I.A. 13 May 1915, leading a charge at Ypres; name on Menin Gate. Poem found in his kit when he died:

"Be Still And Feel The Night"

There is a healing magic in the night,
The breeze blows cleaner than it did by day,
Forgot the fever of the fuller light,
And sorrow sinks insensibly away
As if some saint a cool white hand did lay

Upon the brow, and calm the restless brain.
The moon looks down with pale unpassioned ray -
Sufficient for the hour is its pain.
Be still and feel the night that hides away earth's stain.
Be still and loose the sense of God in you,
Be still and send your soul into the all,
The vasty distance where the stars shine blue,
No longer antlike on the earth to crawl.
Released from time and sense of great and small
Float on the pinions of the Night-Queen's wings;
Soar till the swift inevitable fall
Will draw you back into all the world's small things;
Yet for an hour be one with all escaped things.

Colwyn had a younger brother, a leading Scout commissioner, Capt. Roland Erasmus Phillips, Royal Fusilier. He won the MC for his assault on Hohenzollern Redoubt in April 1916. K.I.A., at Ovillers, Somme, 7 July 1916.

Volunteering as soon as war broke out, in August 1914, Leslie Coulson was posted to Malta, Egypt and Gallipoli, then, 1916, the Western Front. He spent the summer of 1916 on the Somme, but was shot leading the first wave of an attack at Lesboeufs, along with his poet-friend Lt.Todd (see p.82); he died next day, 8 Oct, 2 months after composing 'The Rainbow'

"The Rainbow" - 8 August 1916
by Leslie Coulson - Journalist.

I watch the white dawn gleam,
 To the thunder of hidden guns.
I hear the hot shell scream
Through skies as sweet as a dream
 Where the silver dawnbreak runs.
And stabbing of light
 Scorches the virginal white.
But I feel in my being, the old, high, sanctified thrill,
And I thank the gods that the dawn is beautiful still.

From death that hurtles by
 I crouch in the trench day-long,
 But up to a cloudless sky
 From the ground where our dead men lie
  A brown lark soars in song.
Through the tortured air,
 Rent by the shrapnel's flare,
Over the troubleless dead he carols his fill,
And I thank the gods that the birds are beautiful still.

Where the parapet is low
  And level with the eye
Poppies and cornflowers glow
  And the corn sways to and fro
In a pattern against the sky.
  The gold stalks hide
  Bodies of men who died
Charging at dawn through the dew to be killed or to kill.
I thank the gods that the flowers are beautiful still.

  When night falls dark we creep
    In silence to our dead.
We dig a few feet deep
  And leave them there to sleep -
    But blood at night is red,
  Yes, even at night,
  And a dead man's face is white.
And I dry my hands, that are also trained to kill,
And I look at the stars - for the stars are beautiful still.

"**Night in War Time**" by Walter L Wilkinson
K.I.A. Roclincourt, Arras, 9 April 1917

NIGHT and night's menace: Death hath forged a dart
Of every moment's pause and stealthy pass:
Blind Terror reigns: darkly, as in a glass,
Man's wondering Soul beholds his fearful Heart,
And questions, and is shaken: and, apart,
Light Chance, the harlot-goddess, holding Mass,
Scatters her favours broadcast on the grass
As might a drunkard spill his wares in mart!
Time and sweet Order have forsaken men,
So near Eternal seems the Night's foul sway:
We ask of Life: "Has Chaos come again,
With Ruin, and Confusion, and Decay?"
Yet slowly, surely darkness dies: and then,
Out of the deep night's menace, dawns the Day!

A P Herbert had a busy war: 1914 Ordinary Seaman; 1915 Sub-Lt. Gallipoli; to France, wounded April 1917 at Arras; Sept. 1917 Lt. in navy. Later an MP and distinguished writer.

"Open Warfare"

Men said, 'At last! at last the open battle!
 Now shall we fight unfettered o'er the plain,
No more in catacombs be cooped like cattle,
 Nor travel always in a devious drain!'
They were in ecstasies. But I was damping;
 I like the trench, I have no lives to spare;
And in those catacombs, however cramping,
 You did at least know vaguely where you were.

Ah, happy days in deep well-ordered alleys,
 Where, after dining, probably with wine,
One felt indifferent to hostile sallies,
 And with a pipe meandered round the line;
You trudged along a trench until it ended;
 It led at least to some familiar spot;
It might not be the place that you'd intended,
 But then you might as well be there as not.

But what a wilderness we now inhabit
 Since this confounded 'open' strife prevails!
It may be good; I do not wish to crab it,
 But you should hear the language it entails,
Should see this waste of wide unchartered craters
 Where it is vain to seek the companies,
Seeing the shell-holes are as like as taters
 And no one knows where anybody is.

Oft in the darkness, palpitant and blowing,
 Have I set out and lost the hang of things,
And ever thought, 'Where can the guide be going?'
 But trusted long and rambled on in rings,
For ever climbing up some miry summit,
 And halting there to curse the contrite guide,
For ever then descending like a plummet
 Into a chasm in the other side.

Oft have I sat and wept, or sought to study
 With hopeless gaze the uninstructive stars,
Hopeless because the very skies were muddy;
 I only saw a red malicious Mars;

Or pulled my little compass out and pondered,
 And set it sadly on my shrapnel hat,
Which, I suppose, was why the needle wandered,
 Only, of course, I never thought of that.

And then perhaps some 5.9s start dropping,
 As if there weren't sufficient holes about;
I flounder on, hysterical and sopping,
 And come by chance to where I started out,
And say once more, while I have no objection
 To other people going to Berlin,
Give me a trench, a nice revetted section,
 And let me stay there till the Bosch gives in!

A P Herbert

Lt. G G Samuel, Eton, then worked for Stepney Jewish Lads' Club, and endowed an orphanage. Twice rejected for bad eyesight, then served in Belgium, April 1916 until k.i.a. June 1917, at Messines Ridge.

"Consolation" - by G G Samuel

Oh! I sigh when I think of the men
 In the trenches of Flanders and France;
 And I dream of the days of romance,
 Of the bow and the shield and the lance,
And the chivalrous tales that the pen
Of a poet could celebrate then.
For the brutal inventions of crime
 Are the weapons of battle to-day;
 And the guns that remorselessly slay
 Blow the ramparts and shelters away.
And there in the mud and the slime
Are the heroes who fall in their prime.

Flower left school at 13, was rejected by army, being half an inch too short, so he wrote to Lord Kitchener, & was accepted! Driver in the Artillery, wounded, transferred to Signals. April 1917, shelter in German dug-out at Neuville-St-Vaast. Entrance to dug-out was open to German shelling, (cf. W Owen at Serre in January 1917), and a direct hit killed him and all his pals outright.

"A Calm Night At The Front"

The rough Profanity is lost in sleep,
 The body rests, the mind is dreaming:
The men on guard their watch do keep,
 The moon's rays gently beaming.

The rifle fire has died away
 All silent now; the moon on high
Would set a truce until the day
 God staying the hand of destiny

I think that when those dark'ning clouds
 Have gathered up the tempest's lust
The blackness of the night in shrouds
 Will show how mean the human trust.

The fiend of war that hides in wait
 Will venture forth in boom of guns
And rattling lead a "Hymn of Hate",
 Wild dirge of men - just women's sons.

I do not doubt there is an end
 To all this slaughter of the brave
By monster forms who tear and rend
 The innocent before the grave.

O womenfolk of British lands
 Who toil and sweat in holiest cause
O raise in prayer your clasped hands
 That men may see the curse of wars.

A single starlight held in space
 Has filled the trench with radiance white
A cautious soldier hides his face
 Somebody's calling so "Good Night".

Clifford Flower

Weaving gained a double first at Oxford in Classics and Maths and was mentored in his poetry by Robert Bridges. A schoolmaster, he volunteered as a Lieutenant in 1915, but was evacuated from France with heart failure that September, and discharged.

"Birds in the Trenches"

Ye fearless birds that live and fly where men
Can venture not and live, that even build
Your nests where oft the searching shrapnel shrilled
And conflict rattled like a serpent, when
The hot guns thundered further, and from his den
The little machine-gun spat, and men fell piled
In long-swept lines, as when a scythe has thrilled,
And tall corn tumbled ne'er to rise again.
Ye slight ambassadors twixt foe and foe,
Small parleyers of peace where no peace is,
Sweet disregarders of man's miseries
And his most murderous methods, winging slow
About your perilous nests - we thank you, so
Unconscious of sweet domesticities.

Willoughby Weaving

Four poems by Georg Trakl: A chemist and drug addict, attached to the Austrian Medical Corps in August 1914, as a lieutenant, Trakl broke down after the battle of Grodek and was locked up in Cracow, where he died from an overdose of cocaine, 4 November 1914.

"Klage" - "Lament" by Georg Trakl

Sleep and death - sinister eagles
whirr all night long around this head:
Eternity's freezing wave
would devour the golden image
of man. On horrible reefs
the purple body is shattered
and the dark voice laments
above the seas.
Sister of stormy sadness,
see, a fearful boat is sinking
under stars,
the silent countenance of night.

"Menschheit" - "Mankind" by Georg Trakl

Round gorges deep with fire arrayed, mankind;
A roll of drums, dark brows of warriors marching;
Footsteps in fog of blood, black metals grind;
Despair, sad night of thought, despair high-arching;
Eve's shadow falls, halloo of hunt, red coin consigned.
Cloud, broken by light, the Supper's end;
This bread, this wine, have silence in their keeping.
Here do the Twelve, assembled, numbered, stand;
They cry out under olive trees at night, half sleeping.
Into the wound Saint Thomas dips his hand.

"Im Osten" - "Eastern Front" by Georg Trakl

The wrath of the people is dark,
Like the wild organ notes of winter storm,
The battle's crimson wave, a naked
Forest of stars.

With ravaged brows, with silver arms
To dying soldiers night comes beckoning.
In the shade of the autumn ash
Ghosts of the fallen are sighing.

Thorny wilderness girdles the town about.
From bloody doorsteps the moon
Chases terrified women.
Wild wolves have poured through the gates.

"Grodek" - Georg Trakl's final poem:

At nightfall the autumn woods cry out
With deadly weapons and the golden plains,
The deep blue lakes, above which more darkly
Rolls the sun; the night embraces
Dying warriors, the wild lament
Of their broken mouths.
But quietly there in the willow dell
Red clouds in which an angry god resides,
The shed blood gathers, lunar coolness.
All the roads lead to blackest carrion.
Under golden twigs of the night and stars
The sister's shade now sways through the silent copse
To greet the ghosts of the heroes, the bleeding heads;
And softly the dark flutes of autumn sound in the reeds.
O prouder grief! You brazen altars,
Today a great pain feeds the hot flame of the spirit,
The grandsons yet unborn.

Alfred's last poem, written 15 September 1914, 9 days before he died of wounds at Vermandovillers:

"Die Schlacht Bei Saarburg" - "The Battle Of Saarburg"

The earth is growing mouldy with mist.
The evening is heavy as lead.
Electrical crackling bursts out all round,
And with a whimper everything breaks asunder.

Like old rags
The villages are smouldering on the horizon.
I am lying God-forsaken
In the rattling front-line.

Many enemy copper birds
Whirl around my heart and head.
I brace myself in the greyness
And face death.

Alfred Lichtenstein

Jean-Marc Bernard joined the infantry after 3 attempts (bad eyesight), killed by a shell near Carency, 9 July 1915.

"**De Profundis**" by Jean-Marc Bernard

From the depths of this trench
we raise up our hands
to you Lord: have mercy on us and
on our shrivelled soul!
For even more than our flesh
our soul is weary and without form.
We have been battered by a storm
of rain and steel and ash,
You see us caked with mud
Ripped, haggard, obscene...
But oh our hearts, have you seen?
Yet, my God, one must admit,
we are so bereft of hope,
peace seems so far away
we cannot know from day
to day if we will cope.
Enlighten us in this quagmire,
encourage us and banish
our chafed hearts' anguish.
Ah! Give us back our fire!
But to the dead whose bitter grave
lies here unmarked in sand and clay
give them eternal rest this day,
You know, O Lord, all have deserved it.

At a look-out post on the Meuse, 1915.

"**Nocturne**" by Albert-Paul Granier

The guns have fallen silent, gagged with fog,
in the winter's night that cancels space,
and a calm full of menace,
like the screech of owls over castle walls,
hangs in the many-hearted silence.
Sentries, peering out,
tense every muscle, edgily
awaiting the unexpected.
A thwack like wet cloth
sounds from the valley -
sudden muffled rifle-shots

unsure of guessed-at shadows
and the rustling emptiness.
This is a night
like the nights in Breton legend
when hell-hag washerwomen
kneel invisible at riverside stones,
beating shrouds in the thick water.

Written in Hoogstade Hospital - 11 November 1917. Gaston volunteered for infantry August 1914, aged 18, and fought for four years in the trenches until he trained as a fighter pilot, in March 1918. Shot down and died, 7 October.

"Chansons Ardentes" by Gaston De Ruyter, a Belgian.

By evening's blue-grey threshold stirs a breeze;
And all along the road the bowing trees,
Though gale and tempest now have turned to flight,
Trembled to sense it lost in the dark night.

A breath of trust, tenderly soothing pain,
Has crept about the hollows of the plain.
While raging hearts have quivered in their hate,
A breath of love prompts dreams of happier fate.

As the north wind drove the mills ceaselessly
And death too let its sombre sails turn free,
Frail, lissom women, stooping with bowed head,
Closed for all time the eyelids of the dead.

Ah, hope's bright visions! Spectral wraiths in white,
For your grim work you flock together; then
Your women's, golden, hearts bow day and night
Over long agonies of dying men.

Ah, your hands' gestures and your smiling eyes!
Blue, spectral wraiths beside the beds of pain,
You bring your solace to each man who dies
And reassurance to those who remain!

A breeze has risen in the tempest's train
And steals about the fringes of the plain:
Your breath of tenderness, soft as a sigh,
O women, cools our brows as you pass by!

"Wo Wölfe..."

Where wolves ran through the bright night snow,
The night was full of sudden hunger:
Wild cries filled the air. Long-necked shells
And shrapnel call out.
Iron teeth without lips.
Hotly hungering for my ribs.
In the tension of the snowy light of dawn
We are once again beset by the baying voices of death
Raging towards us with deafening explosions.

Peter Baum

To his friend Felix Braun, in memory of the Spring of 1915

"A Comrade" by Heinrich Lersch

Bravely he stood, endured the long cold winter,
Nerved by the thought that out of war and pain
Best could he serve the land of his devotion,
Win for the world some great and lasting gain.

Only at night, when softly shone the starlight
When o'er the silent sky its radiance spread;
Yearnings for home stirred deep and strong within him,
Thoughts of the homeland as of one long dead.

But when the air was filled with Spring's first sweetness,
Pain drew a veil o'er eyes that once shone clear;
Sleeping he groaned, his stern face pale with longing,
Pale with the dreams of all that makes life dear.

So, when at dawn, the land was filled with bird-song,
Trembling, he stood, his face turned towards the sky,
Where midst the roar and horror of the battle,
Carolled the lark its first glad song on high.

Then burst his soul from out its cramping fetters,
Dumbly he wept, through anguish came to know
Hatred and War, deprived of all their glory,
Futile, inhuman, harbingers of woe.

Nevertheless his arm, which once aimed deadly missiles,
Heedless his ear when called on to obey -
Dreaming, exalted, deaf to noise of battle,

Musing, remote, he stood and dreamed all day;
Fell down and kissed the naked earth beneath him,
Dead to all pain, and heedless of the strife,
Heard no commands, nor sound of shell and cannon,
Heard but the lark which sang of love and life.

Heinrich Lersch
[translated by Sylvia Colenso]

Capt. J E Crombie, son and grandson of MPs, commissioned at 18, on leaving Winchester College; to France February 1915, wounded in April - major operations in England. In November 1916, at Ovillers, he wrote, from the trenches.

"Desolation"

Over the bare, blank line of the ridge,
Over the stump of Sentinel Tree,
The moon slowly crosses the unseen bridge
That is set in the sky from the hills to the sea.

The sun's pale sister, moving yet dead,
The scars show dark on her weary face:
Is it strife of a million years that have bled
Her heart's life, and set Death's frosty sheen in her place?

Is she watching our strife, the tired moon? Can she see
How the earth's face is scarred, her life ebbing fast?
And only the shorn stump of Sentinel Tree
Prays in the silence, "How long will her agony last?"

Like Edward Thomas, Robert Vernède was educated at St.Paul's School, and then Oxford. He was also killed on the same day, 9 April 1917, aged nearly 42. Enlisting, over-age, in 1915-16 he fought in the Ypres Salient and then on the Somme, where he was wounded in the thigh.

"A Listening Post"

The sun's a red ball in the oak
  And the grass is grey with dew,
Awhile ago a blackbird spoke -
  He didn't know the world's askew.

And yonder rifleman and I
  Wait here behind the misty trees
To shoot the first man that goes by,
  Our rifles ready on our knees.

How could he know that if we fail
  The world may lie in chains for years
And England be a bygone tale
  And right be wrong, and laughter tears?

Strange that this bird sits there and sings
  While we must only sit and plan -
Who are so much the higher things -
  The murder of our fellow man ...

But maybe God will cause to be -
  Who brought forth sweetness from the strong -
Out of our discords harmony
  Sweeter than that bird's song.

R. E. Vernède

"Noon"

It is midday: the deep trench glares...
A buzz and blaze of flies...
The hot wind puffs the giddy airs...
The great sun rakes the skies.

No sound in all the stagnant trench
Where forty standing men
Endure the sweat and grit and stench,
Like cattle in a pen.

Sometimes a sniper's bullet whirs
Or twangs the whining wire;
Sometimes a soldier sighs and stirs
As in hell's frying fire.

From out a high cool cloud descends
An aeroplane's far moan...
The sun strikes down, the thin cloud rends...
The black spot travels on.

And sweating, dizzied, isolate
In the hot trench beneath,
We bide the next shrewd move of fate
Be it of life or death.

R. E. Vernède

"September 25, 1916" by F Bendall

I sat on the fire-step – by my side
The adjutant – next him an F.O.O.
The trench was an old German one, reversed
The parapet was made of many things
That should not have been there at all–the time
Was zero minus twenty; and the noise
That had been horrible enough before
Grew to an unimaginable pitch.
It seemed as tho' I had no eyes, no mouth,
No sense of sight, no taste, no power of speech
But only hearing - hearing multiplied
To the last limit of a dizzy brain.
The noise was everywhere about - but mostly
Above us; - and was made of every sort
Of bang, crash, whistle, whine, thump, shriek and thud.
If every devil from the pit of hell,
Each with an unmelodious instrument,
Each vieing with the other in making noise,
Had flown above me in the tortured air,
One great infernal pandemonium,
I do not think they would have made a tenth
Of the long seismic polyphony that passed
Over our heads. I saw the adjutant's
Mouth open, and his lips move as in speech
But no words came that I could hear, because
My hearing was entirely occupied.
The trench wall rocked – then dust and clods of earth
Fell all about me and I was aware
Of fat grey smoke-wreathes and an acrid smell.
And dimly, as one hears a metronome,
In punctuating stabs of sharper sound
Thro' a great orchestrated symphony
I heard the German counter- barrage burst
On the high ground above us, saw my watch
Marking three minutes to the zero hour,
Sat for another unremembered space
Wondering what would happen if a shell
Fell in the trench beside me; felt again
By some sixth sense rather than thro' my ears,
That there were fewer shells - that they had ceased.
Climbed on the parapet - and - north by east
From the torn hill of Ginchy Telegraph -
Saw - aye and seeing cheered exultantly -

The long well-ordered lines of our advance
From Bouleaux Wood to distant Guedecourt
Sweep from the valley underneath my feet
Up the long slopes to Morval and Les Boeufs.

by F W D Bendall

"**Ballade**" - Mauquissart, January 1917

In days of knightly pride
To meet a knightly foe
Baron and squire would ride
In mail -- a gallant show
The stirrup cup would flow
The vizor'd casque they'd don
Now is it thus? Ah no
The pomp of war is gone.

With lance and sword well tried
From donjon or chateau
They galloped side by side
Plumes in a crested row
Thus chivalry would go;
But we are fallen on
Days that have lost their glow
The pomp of war is gone.

The light of day denied
By devious ways below
We crawl and slink and slide
Our days are long and slow,
In mud and filth, and woe
Deep-marked on faces wan.
For Science speaks, and lo–
The pomp of war is gone.

Envoi
Princess, you would not know
That once our buttons shone!
But -- courage stays -- alto'
The pomp of war is gone.

by F W D Bendall

"Outposts"

Sentry, sentry, what did you see
At gaze from post beside Lone Tree?
A star-shell flared like a burning brand
But I saw no movement in No Man's Land.
Sentry, sentry, what did you hear
As the night-wind fluttered the grasses near?
I heard a rifle-shot on the flank,
And my mate slid down to the foot of the bank.

Sentry, sentry, what did you do?
And hadn't your mate a word for you?
I lifted his head and called his name.
His lips moved once, but no sound came.
Sentry, sentry, what did you say
As you watched alone till break of day?
I prayed the Lord that I'd fire straight
If I saw the man that killed my mate.

Frederic W D Bendall

"The German Dug-Out"

Forty feet down
A room dug out of the clay,
Roofed and strutted and tiled complete;
The floor still bears the mark of feet
(Feet that never will march again!)
The door-post's edge is rubbed and black
(Shoulders that never will lift a pack
Stooping through the wind and rain!)
Forty feet down from the light of day
Forty feet down.

Ago
Sixteen men lived there,
Lived, and drank, and slept, and swore,
Smoked, and shivered, and cursed the war,
Wrote to the people at home maybe,
While the rafters shook to the thudding guns;
Husbands, fathers, and only sons,
Sixteen fellows like you and me
Lived in that cavern twelve feet square
A week ago.

Into the dark
Did a cry ring out on the air
Or died they stiffly and unafraid
In the crash and flame of the hand-grenade?
We took the trench and its mounded dead,
And the tale of their end is buried deep,
A secret which sixteen corpses keep
With the sixteen souls which gasped and fled
Up forty steps of battered stair,

Into the dark.
Forty feet down,
Veiled from the decent sky,
The clay of them turns to its native clay,
And the stench is a blot on the face of the day.
Men are a murderous breed, it seems,
And these, maybe, are quieter so;
Their spirits have gone where such things go;
Nor worms nor wars can trouble their dreams;
And their sixteen twisted bodies lie
Forty feet down.

by J L C Brown

"**Tears**" by Osbert Sitwell

Silence o'erwhelms the melody of Night,
Then slowly drips onto the woods that sigh
For their past vivid vernal ecstasy.
The branches and the leaves let in the light
In patterns, woven 'gainst the paler sky
- Create mysterious Gothic tracery,
Between those high dark pillars, - that affright
Poor weary mortals who are wandering by.
Silence drips on the woods like sad faint rain,
Making each frail tired sigh, a sob of pain:
Each drop that falls, a hollow painted tear
Such as are shed by Pierrrots, when they fear
Black clouds may crush their silver lord to death.
The world is waxen; and the wind's least berth
Would make a hurricane of sound. The earth
Smells of the hoarded sunlight that gave birth
To the gold-glowing radiance of that leaf,
Which falls to bury from our sight its grief.

NO MAN'S LAND

A. P. Herbert's unit was almost obliterated at Beaucourt: of 435 men who attacked, only 20 were fit to fight the following day, of which two officers. Friend William Ker was killed the first day, 13 Nov 1916. Herbert was one of the lucky twenty, and later revisited:-

"Beaucourt Revisited"

I wandered up to Beaucourt; I took the river track,
And saw the lines we lived in before the Boche went back;
But Peace was now in Pottage, the front was far ahead,
The front had journeyed Eastward, and only left the dead.
And I thought, how long we lay there, and watched across the wire,
While guns roared round the valley, and set the skies afire!
But now there are homes in HAMEL and tents in the Vale of Hell,
And a camp at suicide corner, where half a regiment fell.
The new troops follow after, and tread the land we won,
To them 'tis so much hill-side re-wrested from the Hun;
We only walk with reverence this sullen mile of mud;
The shell-holes hold our history, and half of them our blood.
Here, at the head of Peche Street, 'twas death to show your face;
To me it seemed like magic to linger in the place;
For me how many spirits hung around the Kentish Caves,
But the new men see no spirits – they only see the graves.
I found the half-dug ditches we fashioned for the fight,
We lost a score of men there – young James was killed that night;
I saw the star shells staring, I heard the bullets hail,
But the new troops pass unheeding – they never heard the tale.
I crossed the blood-red ribbon, that once was No-Man's Land,
I saw a misty daybreak and a creeping minute-hand;
And here the lads went over, and there was Harmsworth shot,
And here was William lying – but the new men know them not.
And I said, "There is still the river, and still the stiff, stark trees,
To treasure here our story, but there are only these";
But under the white wood crosses the dead men answered low,
"The new men know not BEAUCOURT, but we are here – we know."

A. P. Herbert

"During The Bombardment" by T P Cameron Wilson

What did we know of birds?
Though the wet woods rang with their blessing,
And the trees were awake and aware with wings,
And the little secrets of mirth, that have no words,
Made even the brambles chuckle, like baby things
Who find their toes too funny for any expressing.

What did we know of flowers?
Though the fields were gay with their flaming
Poppies, like joy itself, burning the young green maize,
And spreading their crinkled petals after the showers -
Cornflower vieing with mustard; all the three of them shaming
The tired old world with its careful browns and greys.

What did we know of summer,
The larks, and the dusty clover,
And the little furry things that were busy and starry-eyed?
Each of us wore his brave disguise, like a mummer,
Hoping that no one saw, when the shells came over,
The little boy who was funking - somewhere inside!

Three evocations of Night Patrols in No Man's Land:

Lt. James Reese Europe, a band leader and the first black American officer in France and the first to lead an attack, in 1918. Wounded by gas, he wrote this poem, and its music, while recuperating in hospital:

"On Patrol in No Man's Land"

What's the time? nine? all in line
Alright boys now take it slow
Are you ready? Steady!
Very good Eddy.
Over the top let's go
Quiet, sly it, else you'll start a riot
Keep your proper distance, follow 'long
Cover smother when you see me hover
Obey my orders and you won't go wrong
There's a minnenwerfer coming, look out (Bang!)
Hear that roar, there's one more.
Stand fast, there's a Very Light -
Don't gasp or they'll find you alright -
Don't start to bombing with those hand grenades

There's a machine gun, Holy Spades!
Alert, Gas! Put on your masks -
A-just it correctly and hurry up fast -
Drop! There's a rocket for the Boche Barrage,
Down, hug the ground close as you can, don't stand,
Creep and crawl, follow me, that's all -
What do you hear? Nothing near, all is clear don't fear,
That's the life of a stroll when you take a patrol -
Out in No Man's Land!
Ain't it grand?
Out in No Man's Land.

by James Reese Europe

J R Europe was a very famous band-leader, and was charged with making the Harlem Hellfighters the best military band in the US Army. He combined concerts with machine-gun fighting. If you wish to hear Europe singing his own song, go to "http://syncopatedtimes.com" and click on the poem's title.

"In No Man's Land" by Ewart Alan Mackintosh MC

The hedge on the left, and the trench on the right,
And the whispering, rustling wood between,
And who knows where in the wood tonight
Death or capture may lurk unseen,
The open field and the figures lying
Under the shade of the apple trees -
Is it wind in the branches sighing,
Or a German trying to stop a sneeze?
Louder the voices of night come thronging,
But over them all the sound is clear,
Taking me back to the place of my longing
And the cultured sneezes I used to hear
Lecture-time and my tutor's "handker"
Stopping his period's rounded close,
Like the frozen hand of the German ranker
Down in a ditch with a cold in his nose.
I'm cold too, and a stealthy snuffle
From the man with a pistol covering me,
And the Boche moving off with a snap and a shuffle
Break the windows of memory -
I can't make sure till the moon gets lighter -
Anyway shooting is over-bold.
Oh, damn you, get back to your trench, you blighter,
I really can't shoot a man with a cold.

Hammerhead Wood, Thiepval, 1915

On 8th August 1916 there was a Battalion order "A Patrol will leave tonight to examine gap in German wire at C15 b 8.2".

"No Man's Land" - Robert Beckh

Nine-Thirty o'clock? Then over the top,
And mind to keep down when you see the flare
Of Very pistol searching the air.
Now, over you get; look out for the wire
In the borrow pit and the empty tins,
They are meant for the Hun to bark his shins.
So keep well down and reserve your fire–
All over? Right: there's a gap just here
In the corkscrew wire, so just follow me;
If you keep well down there's nothing to fear.

Then out we creep thro' the gathering gloom
Of NO MAN'S LAND, while the big guns boom
Right over our heads, and the rapid crack
Of the Lewis guns is answered back
By the German barking the same refrain
Of crack, crack, crack, all over again.
To the wistful eye from the parapet,
In the smiling sun of a summer's day,
'Twere a sin to believe that a bloody death
In those waving grasses lurking lay.
But now, 'neath the Very's fitful flares
"Keep still, my lads, and freeze like hares;–
All right, carry on, for we're out to enquire
If our friend the Hun's got a gap in his wire;
And he hasn't invited us out, you see,
So lift up your feet and follow me."

Then, silent, we press with a noiseless tread
Thro' no man's land, but the sightless dead;
Aye, muffle your footsteps, well ye may,
For the mouldering corpses here decay.
Oh breathe a prayer for the sightless Dead
Who have bitten the dust 'neath the biting lead
Of the pitiless hail of the Maxim's fire,
'Neath the wash of shell in the well trod mire.
Ah well! But we've, too, got a job to be done,
For we've come to the wire of our friend, the Hun.
"Now, keep well down, lads; can you see any gap?"

Not much, well the reference is wrong in the map"
So homeward we go thro' the friendly night.
That covers the NO MAN'S LAND from sight,
As muttering a noiseless prayer of praise,
We drop from the parapet into the bays.

"Left Alone" by Dudley H Harris

Left alone among the dying!
All around are moaning, sighing
Or are cursing, sobbing, crying
In Death's crushing hushing hand.
We are torn upon the wire,
We are scorched and burnt with fire,
Or lie choking in the mire
Of the star-lit "No Man's Land".
Hear our prayers, O! gentle Jesus,
Send Thine angels down to ease us
From the pains of Hell that seize us,
From our burning, yearning thirst.
We are broken, we are battered,
Bodies twisted, crushed and shattered
By the shells and bullets scattered
On this strip of land accurst.
Round about are shadows creeping
Formless Things which wake the sleeping,
Glaring eyes from shell-holes peeping
Mocking always at our pain.
Cold and wet our limbs are numbing,
Fevered brows are drumming, drumming -
Are the stretchers never coming?
Are we numbered with the slain?
God in Heaven, canst Thou hear us?
Mary Mother! Dost Thou fear us?
Stretcher-bearers, are you near us?
  Give us water or we die!
But a grisly shadow's creeping
With his cruel scythe a-reaping
Weary souls which fall to sleeping
  In a choking, croaking sigh.

D H H - 1917

"**Tom**" by Digby B Haseler

Tom he lay in No Man's Land with a bloody broken thigh,
Tom lay out among the wire and stared up at the sky.
The sun beat down like fire of hell and the earth was brown and dry.

Tom shouted out for water while the earth called out for rain,
And six good men went out to try and bring him in again,
And six good men lie deaf and blind upon that bloody plain.

But the Boche they wouldn't shoot Tom, they liked to see him lie
Calling "Christ!" with burning lips and staring at the sky.
So Tom lay in No Man's Land until he had to die.

Digby B. Haseler

Peter Baum, a German stretcher-bearer, killed in June 1916 by shrapnel, aged 46.

"Leuchtkugeigen Steigen..."

Flares climb high up into the sky,
Fireworks extending the night and the sputtering light
Of a decaying moon. With your gun you stand there rigid
As the houses that are lit up.
Flares of bristling tiger's fur.
A trigger is lying in wait for any movement revealed by light
To watchful eye, as though the day
Were not yet dead in which one man was another's prey,
One man's mouth at another's throat,
Until the organ-cry of death is heard.
With eyes wide open you stare at the brilliance
Of the colourful predator, burning brightly in the night.
Until night and snow conceal me again,
Grey-green eyes keep these wild melodies awake.

Peter Baum

"Brüder / Brothers" by Heinrich Lersch, 1915

Es lag schon lang ein Toter vor unserm Drahtverhau #

Before our wire there lay for long a dead man full in view #
The sun burned down upon him, he was cooled by wind and dew.

Each day that passed I stared at him, and strained to see his face
And ever felt more certain; my brother lay in that place.

And often as I looked at him, outstretched before my gaze,
I seemed to hear his merry voice from far-off peaceful days.

And in my dreams I heard him crying out and weeping sore,
"Ah, brother, dearest brother, do you love me then no more?"

At last I risked the bullets and the shrapnel-rain, and ran
And fetched him in, and buried ... an unknown fellow-man.

My eyes, they did deceive me. -- My heart it knew its place:
For, on every fallen soldier, I see my brother's face. ¢

Es hat ein jeder Toter des Bruders Angesicht. ¢

Osbert Sitwell, celebrated man of letters and prolific author, enlisted in the Grenadier Guards, 1912-19, aged 19, and served the whole war, mainly near Ypres, leaving as a Captain. He started composing poetry then; this, his first effort, could well be a description of the ruined Ypres:

"Babel"

Therefore is the name of it called Babel

by Osbert Sitwell

And still we stood and stared far down
Into that ember-glowing town
Which every shaft and shock of fate
Had shorn into its base. Too late
Came carelessly Serenity.
Now torn and broken houses gaze
On the rat-infested maze
That once sent up rose-silver haze
To mingle through eternity.
The outlines, once so strongly wrought,
Of city walls, are now a thought
Or jest unto the dead who fought...
Foundation for futurity.
The shimmering sands where once there played
Children with painted pail and spade
Are drearly desolate, — afraid
To meet Night's dark humanity,
Whose silver cool remakes the dead,
And lays no blame on any head
For all the havoc, fire, and lead,
That fell upon us suddenly.
When all we came to know as good
Gave ways to Evil's fiery flood,
And monstrous myths of iron and blood
Seem to obscure God's clarity.
Deep sunk in sin, this tragic star
Sinks deeper still, and wages war
Against itself; strewn all the seas
With victims of a world disease.
- And we are left to drink the lees
Of Babel's direful prophecy.

BEHIND THE LINES

Ivor Gurney's empathy with Nature.

"Communion"

Beauty lies so deep
On all the fields,
Nothing for the eyes
But blessing yields.

Tall elms, greedy for light,
Stand tip-toe. See
The last light linger in
Their tracery.

The guns are dumb, are still
All evil noises.
The singing heart in peace
Softly rejoices.

Only unsatisfied
With Beauty's hunger
And sacramental thirst -
Nothing of anger.

Mist wraiths haunt the path
As daylight lessens,
The stars grow clearer, and
My dead friend's presence.

Ivor Gurney - January 1917

The ugliness of War is too painful to bear.

"Pain"

Pain, pain continual, pain unending;
Hard even to the roughest, but to those
Hungry for beauty .. Not the wisest knows,
Nor most pitiful-hearted, what the wending
Of one hour's way meant. Gray monotony lending
Weight to the gray skies, gray mud where goes
An army of gray bedrenched scarecrows in rows
Careless at last of cruellest Fate-sending.

Seeing the pitiful eyes of men foredone,
Or horses shot, too tired merely to stir,
Dying in shell-holes both, slain by the mud.
Men broken, shrieking even to hear a gun. -
Till pain grinds down, or lethargy numbs her,
The amazed heart cries angrily out on God.
Somme or Crucifix Corner - Ivor Gurney, Feb. 1917

"**Præmaturi**" by Margaret P Cole

When men are old, and their friends die,
They are not so sad,
Because their love is running slow,
And cannot spring from the wound with so sharp a pain;
And they are happy with many memories,
And only a little while to be alone.
But we are young, and our friends are dead
Suddenly, and our quick love is torn in two;
So our memories are only hopes that came to nothing.
We are left alone like old men; we should be dead
But there are years and years in which we will still be young.

"**The Monstrous Regiment**" by Alice Coats

What hosts of women everywhere I see!
I'm sick to death of them - and they of me.
(The few remaining men are small and pale -
War lends a spurious value to the male.)
Mechanics are supplanted by their mothers
Aunts take the place of artisans and others;
Wives sell the sago, daughters drive the van,
Even the mansion is without a man!
Females are farming who were frail before,
Matrons attending meeting by the score,
Maidens are minding multiple machines,
And virgins vending station-magazines.
Dames, Hoydens, wenches, harridans and hussies
Cram to congestion all the trams and buses;
Misses and grandmas, mistresses and nieces,
Infest bombed buildings picking up the pieces.
Girls from the South and lassies from the North,
Sisters and sweethearts bustle back and forth.
The newsboy and the boy who drives the plough:
Postman and milkman - all are ladies now.

Doctors and engineers - yes, even these -
Poets and politicians, all are shes.
(The very beasts that in the meadows browse
Are ewes and mares, heifers and hens and cows...)
All, doubtless, worthy to a high degree;
But oh, how boring! Yes, including me.

Carola Oman was a friend of fellow poet May Wedderburn Cannan, both daughters of Oxford academics.

1 July 1916 - Oman became a VAD nurse with British Red Cross in Oxford; April 1917, posted to France. While stationed in Boulogne & Wimereux, September 1918 - January 1919, she wrote these 3 poems:

"In The Ypres Sector"

You have left beauty here in everything
And it is we that are both deaf and blind.
By coarse grass mounds here the small crosses rise
Sunk sideways in the ditch, or low inclined
Over some little stream where waters sing
By shell holes blue with beauty from the skies.
Even the railway cutting has kind shade
And colour, where the rusty wire is laid
Round the soft tracks. Because you knew them thus
The dark-mouthed dug-outs hold a light for us.
And here each name rings rich upon our ears
Which first we learnt with sorrow and with tears.

Carola Oman

"Unloading Ambulance Train"

Into the siding very wearily
She comes again:
Singing her endless song so drearily,
The midnight winds sink down to drift the rain.

So she comes home once more.

Is it an ancient chanty
Won from some classic shore?
The stretcher-bearers stand
Two on either hand.
They bend and lift and raise

Where the doors open wide
With yellow light ablaze.
Into the dark outside
Each stretcher passes. Here
(As if each on his bier
With sorrow they were bringing)
Is peace, and a low singing.

The ambulances load,
Move on and take the road.
Under the stars alone
Each stretcher passes out.
And the ambulances' moan
And the checker's distant shout
All round to the old sound
Of the last chanty singing.
And the dark seamen swinging.
Far off some classic shore...

So, home once more.

Carola Oman, Wimereux, September 1918

"The Armistice" by May Wedderburn Cannan
In an office, in Paris

The news came through over the telephone
All the terms had been signed: the War was won:
And all the fighting and the agony
And all the labour of the years were done.
One girl clicked sudden at her typewriter
And whispered 'Jerry's safe' and sat and stared:
One said, 'It's over, over, it's the end:
The War is over: ended': and a third,
'I can't remember life without the war.'
And one came in and said, 'Look here, they say
We can all go at five to celebrate.
As long as two stay on, just for today.'
It was quite quiet in the big empty room
Among the typewriters and little piles
Of index cards: one said, 'We'd better just
Finish the day's reports and do the files.'
And said, 'It's awf'lly like Recessional,

Now when the tumult has all died away."
The other said, 'Thank God we saw it through;
I wonder what they'll do at home today.'
And said, 'You know it will be quiet tonight
Up at the Front: first time in all these years.
And no one will be killed there any more,'
And stopped, to hide her tears.
She said 'I've told you; he was killed in June.'
"The other said, 'My dear, I know; I know ...
It's over for me too ... My man was killed,
Wounded and died, at Ypres ... three years ago ...
And he's my Man, and I want him,' she said,
And knew that peace could not give back her Dead.

11 November 1918

May Wedderburn Cannan, Carola Oman's Oxford friend, was head of MI5's Espionage Section in Paris at the end of the war.

"G lifted her glass to me and said 'Absent'. I did not know her story, nor she mine, but I drank to my friends who were dead." ['G' was May's colleague.]

"Paris, November 11 1918" - For G.A.H.

Down on the boulevards the crowds went by,
The shouting and the singing died away,
And in the quiet we rose to drink the toasts,
Our hearts uplifted to the hour, the day;
The King - the Army - Navy - the Allies - England - and Victory. -
And then you turned to me and with low voice
(The tables were abuzz with revelry)
'I have a toast for you and me,' you said,
And whispered 'Absent,' and we drank
Our unforgotten Dead.
But I saw Love go lonely down the years,
And when I drank, the wine was salt with tears.

M W Cannan

"For a Survivor of the Mesopotamian Campaign"

War's wasted era is a desert shore,
As know those who have passèd there, a place
Where, within sound of swoll'n destruction's roar,
Wheel the wild vultures, lust and terror base;
Where, making ready for them, stalk the grim
Barbarian forms, hunger, disease and pain,
Who, slashing all life's beauty limb from limb,
Crush it as folly on the stony plain.
A desert: – those too who, as thou, have been
Followers of war's angel, Sacrifice,
(Stern striders to beyond brute torment's scene,
Soarers above the swerves of fear and vice)
Know that the lightning of his ghostly gaze
Has wrecked for them for ever earth's small ways.

by Elizabeth Daryush

"June, 1915"

Who thinks of June's first rose today?
Only some child, perhaps, with shining eyes and rough bright hair
will reach it down.
In a green sunny lane, to us almost as far away
As are the fearless stars from these veiled lamps of town.

What's little June to a great broken world with eyes gone dim
From too much looking on the face of grief, the face of dread?
Or what's the broken world to June and him
Of the small eager hand, the shining eyes, the rough bright head?

by Charlotte Mew

"The German Ward" by Vera Brittain

('inter arma caritas')
When the years of strife are over and my recollection fades
  Of the wards wherein I worked the weeks away,
I shall still see, as a vision rising mid the War-time shades,
  The ward in France where German wounded lay.

I shall see the pallid faces and the half-suspicious eyes,
  I shall hear the bitter groans and laboured breath,
And recall the loud complaining and the weary tedious cries,
And sights and smells of blood and wounds and death.

I shall see the convoy cases, blanket-covered on the floor,
  And watch the heavy stretcher-work begin,
And the gleam of knives and bottles through the open theatre door,
  And the operation patients carried in.

I shall see the Sister standing, with her form of youthful grace,
  And the humour and the wisdom of her smile,
And the tale of three years' warfare on her thin expressive face
  The weariness of many a toil-filled while.

I shall think of how I worked for her with nerve and heart and mind,
  And marvelled at her courage and her skill,
And how the dying enemy her tenderness would find
  Beneath her scornful energy of will.

And I learnt that human mercy turns alike to friend or foe
  When the darkest hour of all is creeping nigh,
And those who slew our dearest, when their lamps were burning low,
  Found help and pity ere they came to die.

So, though much will be forgotten when the sound of War's alarms
  And the days of strife and death have passed away,
I shall always see the vision of Love working amidst arms
  In the ward wherein the wounded prisoners lay.

PATRIOTISM & SACRIFICE : GOD & DEATH

War poems by a private soldier, Ivor Gurney, written in the trenches, published in the autumn of 1917, but nearly all composed in 1916. As he was in France all this time, the editing negotiations with printers Sidgwick & Jackson were conducted by Marion Scott. From his first book, entitled "Severn And Somme":

"To Certain Comrades"

To E.S. and J.H. - Ivor's friends, Privates E Skillern & J Hall

Living we loved you, yet withheld our praises
Before your faces;
And though we had your spirits high in honour,
After the English manner
We said no word. yet, as such comrades would,
You understood.
Such friendship is not touched by Death's disaster
But stands the faster;
And all the shocks and trials of time cannot
Shake it one jot.
Beside the fire at night some far December,
We shall remember
And tell men, unbegotten as yet, the story
Of your sad glory -
Of your plain strength, your truth of heart, your splendid
Coolness, all ended!
All ended, ... yet the aching hearts of lovers
Joy overcovers,
Glad in their sorrow; hoping that if they must
Come to the dust,
An ending such as yours may be their portion,
And great good fortune -
That if we may not live to serve in peace
England, watching increase -
Then death with you, honoured, and swift, and high;
And so - not die.

Ivor Gurney

Both men were killed in action - 21 June 1916. Poem composed in the trenches 5 July 1916.

Ivor commits his life to the Will of God

"Serenity"

Nor steel nor flame has any power on me,
Save that its malice work the Almighty Will,
Nor steel nor flame has any power on me;
Through tempests of hell-fire I must go free
And unafraid; so I remember still
Nor steel nor flame has any power on me,
Save that its malice work the Almighty Will.

28 August 1916

"Acquiescence"

Since I can neither alter my destiny
By one hair's breadth from its appointed course;
Since bribes nor prayers nor any earthly force
May from its pathway move a life not free -
I must gather together the whole strength of me,
My senses make my willing servitors;
Cherish and feed the better, starve the worse;
Turn all my pride to proud humility.
Meeting the daily shocks and frozen, stony,
Cynical face of doubt with smiles and joy -
As a battle with autumn winds delights a boy,
Before the smut of the world and the lust of money,
Power, and fame, can yet his youth destroy;
Ere he has scorned his Father's patrimony.

"Requiem I"

Put out your light, O stars, and do not hold
  Your loveliest shining from earth's outworn shell -
Pure and cold your radiance, pure and cold
  My dead friend's face as well.

"Requiem II"

Nor grief nor tears should wrong the silent dead
  Save England's, for her children fallen so far
From her eager care; though by God's justice led
  And fallen in such a war.

"Requiem III"

Pour out your bounty, moon of radiant shining
 On all this shattered flesh, these quiet forms;
For these were slain, so strangely still reclining,
 In the noblest cause was ever waged with arms.

8 November 1916

"Purple and Black"

The death of princes is
 Honoured most greatly,
Proud kings put purple on
 In manner stately.
Though they have lived such life
 As God offends,
Gone fearful down to death,
 Sick, without friends.
And in the temple dim,
 Trumpets of gold
Proclaim their glory; so
 Their story is told.
In sentimental hymns
 Weeping her dolour,
The mother of heroes wears
 Vile black - Death's colour,
Who should walk proudly with
 The noblest one
Of all that purple throng -
 "This was my son."

I.G. 7 January 1917

"Song and Pain"

Out of my sorrow have I made these songs,
 Out of my sorrow;
Though somewhat of the making's eager pain
 From Joy did borrow.
Some day, I trust, God's purpose of Pain for me
 Shall be complete,
And then - to enter the House of Joy ....
 Prepare, my feet.

I.G. Crucifix Corner, 7 January 1917

"A Christmas Prayer from the Trenches 1915"

by Cyril Winterbotham, k.i.a. 27 August 1916 at Ovillers - on Thiépval Memorial

Not yet for us may Christmas bring
Good-will to men, and peace;
In our dark sky no angels sing,
Not yet the great release
For men, when war shall cease.

So must the guns our carols make,
Our gifts must bullets be,
For us no Christmas bells shall wake;
These ruined homes shall see
No Christmas revelry.

In hardened hearts we fain would greet
The Babe at Christmas born,
But lo, He comes with pierced feet,
Wearing a crown of thorn, -
His side a spear has torn.

For tired eyes are all too dim
Our hearts too full of pain,
Our ears too deaf to hear the hymn
Which angels sing in vain,
'The Christ is born again.'

O Jesus, pitiful, draw near
That even we may see
The Little Child who knew not fear;
Thus would we picture Thee
Unmarred by agony.

O'er death and pain triumphant yet
Bid Thou Thy harpers play,
That we may hear them, and forget
Sorrow and all dismay,
And welcome Thee to stay
With us on Christmas Day.

Cyril Winterbotham

Siegfried Sassoon's diary: 26 December 1915

"Christmas night was jolly, by the log fire, the village
full of maudlin sergeants and paralysed privates."

"The Prince of Wounds" - 27 December 1915

The Prince of wounds is with us here;
Wearing his crown he gazes down,
Sad and forgiving and austere.
We have renounced our lovely things,
Music and colour and delight:
The spirit of Destruction sings
And tramples on the flaring night.
But Christ is here upon the cross,
Bound to a road that's dark with blood,
Guarding immitigable loss.
Have we the strength to strive alone
Who can no longer worship Christ?
Is he a God of wood and stone,
While those who served him writhe and moan,
On warfare's altar sacrificed?

Siegfried Sassoon

"That Which Remaineth"

Written 16 July 1918, in memory of Captain E.H. Brittain, MC, k.i.a. on the Asiago Plateau, 15 June 1918

Only the thought of a merry smile,
The wistful dreaming of sad brown eyes -
A brave young warrior, face aglow
With the light of a lofty enterprise.

Only the hope of a gallant heart,
The steady strife for a deathless crown,
In Memory's treasures, radiant now
With the dream of a goal beyond renown.

Only the tale of a dream fulfilled,
A strenuous day and a well-fought fight,
A fearless leader who laughed at Death,
And the fitting end of a gentle knight.

Only a Cross on a mountain side,
The close of a journey short and rough,
A sword laid down and a stainless shield -
No more - and yet, it is not enough!

Vera Brittain

Born in London in 1883, the Marjorie Pickthall moved to Canada when she was seven, returning in 1912; then again to Canada in 1920. A prolific writer from an early age, her ill health led to an early death in 1922, aged 38.

"Marching Men" by Marjorie Pickthall

Under the level winter sky
I saw a thousand Christs go by.
They sang an idle song and free
As they went up to calvary.

Careless of eye and coarse of lip,
They marched in holiest fellowship.
That heaven might heal the world, they gave
Their earth-born dreams to deck the grave.

With souls unpurged and steadfast breath
They supped the sacrament of death.
And for each one, far off, apart,
Seven swords have rent a woman's heart.

Ferenc Békássy was a bi-lingual poet from Hungary. Educated, along with his 5 siblings, at Bedales School, he then read History at King's Cambridge, 1911-1914; he was a friend of Maynard Keynes, Rupert Brooke, and of Frances Cornford, who wrote this poem as a tribute to him:

"Feri Békássy"

We who must grow old and staid,
Full of wisdom, much afraid,
In our hearts like flowers keep
Love for you until we sleep.

You the brave, and you the young
You of a thousand songs unsung,
Burning brain, and ardent word,
You the lovely and absurd.

Say, on that Galician plain
Are you arguing again?
Does a trench or ruined tree
Hear your - 'O, I don't agree!'

We who must grow staid and old,
Full of caution, worn and cold,
In our hearts, like flowers keep
Your image, till we also sleep.
Frances Cornford - 1915

Robert Beckh planned to become a priest and serve in India. To Jesus, Cambridge 1913, joined up as a private Aug 1914. The day after composing this poem, 15 August 1916, Beckh led two patrols in No Man's Land, but was killed by machine-gun fire.

"Billets"

Green fields that are scented and sweet,
God's sunshine, the air, and the trees,
Thy beauties we knew not before,
They were there, and who doubts them that sees?
But we, who bereft for a space
Of the joys that God meant us to share,
Have been living 'mid sandbags, and scorched
Without shade from the sun's ceaseless glare.

Great God! How to welcome the day
When the Trenches are left, and the trees
Promise hopes of a respite from heat,
And from breath-stifling odours release.
For how long? Just four days is the span:
And how fleeting yet heav'n born it seems–
Then again to the Trenches, our goal
And to plan for the Peace of our dreams.
Robert Beckh - 1916

"Who Made The Law?" - by Leslie Coulson

Who made the Law that men should die in meadows?
Who spake the word that blood should splash in lanes?
Who gave it forth that gardens should be bone-yards?
Who spread the hills with flesh, and blood, and brains?
Who made the Law?

Who made the Law that Death should stalk the village?
Who spake the word to kill among the sheaves,
Who gave it forth that death should lurk in hedgerows,
Who flung the dead among the fallen leaves?
Who made the Law?

Those who return shall find that peace endures,
Find old things old, and know the things they knew,
Walk in the garden, slumber by the fireside,
Share the peace of dawn, and dream amid the dew
Those who return.

Those who return shall till the ancient pastures,
Clean-hearted men shall guide the plough-horse reins,
Some shall grow apples and flowers in the valleys,
Some shall go courting in summer down the lanes –
THOSE WHO RETURN.

But who made the Law? the Trees shall whisper to him:
"See, see the blood – the splashes on our bark!"
Walking the meadows, he shall hear bones crackle,
And fleshless mouths shall gibber in silent lanes at dark.
Who made the Law?

Who made the Law? At noon upon the hillside
His ears shall hear a moan, his cheeks shall feel a breath,
And all along the valleys, past gardens, crofts, and homesteads,
He who made the Law shall walk along with Death.

His application for a commission declined, Coulson enlisted in the Royal Fusiliers, served in Egypt, Gallipoli and the Western Front. Killed 8 October 1916, aged 27. This poem was written a few days before he died.

"What is War?" by J. M. Rose-Troup

What is war?
Ask the young men who fight,
Men who defend the right,
Ask them—what is war?
"Honour—or death—that is war,"
Say the young men.

What is war?
Ask of the women who weep,
Mourning for those who sleep,
Ask them—what is war?
"Sorrow and grief—that is war,"
Say the women.

What is war?
By ways beyond our ken,
God tries the souls of men,
Sends retribution just,
Punishing vice and lust,
God's wrath for sin—that is war.

After the war, Rose-Troup worked in the War Office and later as a director of the BBC.

Cpt. E Wilkinson was wounded by grenades at Thiepval, 1 July 1916, and recuperated in Chatham hospital. Returning, he was gassed at Nieuport, 1917, and convalescing again, he wrote:

"France" (August 1917)

Her head unbowed, her knee unbent,
  Her sad, proud eyes unfaltering,
Her white robe soiled and stained and rent,
  Her red sword-point unwavering.

Her banner in her strong left hand,
  Unconquered, free as Freedom, waves;
She stands amidst her ruined land,
  Her broken homes her children's graves.

Her mighty heart beats firm, although
  Her breast with patriot blood is wet,
And victory shall find her so,
  Heroic and undaunted yet.

E Wilkinson

"A Song Of The Sandbags" by Robert Service

No, Bill, I'm not a-spooning out no patriotic tosh
(The cove be'ind the sandbags ain't a death-or-glory cuss).
And though I strafes 'em good and 'ard I doesn't 'ate the Boche,
I guess they're mostly decent, just the same as most of us.
I guess they loves their 'omes and kids as much as you or me;
And just the same as you or me they'd rather shake than fight;
And if we'd 'appened to be born at Berlin-on-the-Spree,
We'd be out there with 'Ans and Fritz, dead sure that we was right.

Lt. Franz Janowitz - *After university in Leipzig & Vienna, Janowitz joined the army in 1913. He was hit by machine-gun fire during an attack; he died 4 Nov. 1917.*

"Sei, Erde, Wahr!" - **"Be, Earth, True!"**

So let this comfort as madness be contrite
that greets the universe with distant light,

For do you not shine gentle, gloomy star,
the inspiring goal of human life so far?
Don't you look kindly through night's loving twigs?
Cover in shining, what makes fear grow big?

Swear not by us, who are removed from earth,
not to this star, when it enjoyed your worth!

You star of war, now cover up your flood,
rise up in spheres as a ball of blood!

As smoking, as you smoke, appear in shame!
Hang out your sign, let murder be your name!

A raging eye, you gaze on nothingness,
to every child of light you bring distress.

A wandering sign announcing mothers' woe,
you at the head, the world must die below.

Prove fatal at each birth, breasts rent by fire!
Be lamp at every kill, and sole desire!

Then, mirrored in a puddle, see him pall,
renouncing drink, the knowing animal!
But if some Being should sense earth's living days,

if he be real, let him lament our ways!

Be, earth, true to the form that we disgrace,
and be - for how could we! - a child of space!

One day, a light will streak. But what is meant?
A joying flash will cross the firmament.

The fields of heaven shine, from terror free.
Man stands and stares, amazed at what can be.
F Janowitz. - 1916

Albert-Paul Granier - *Two poems by a solicitor from Nantes, a pianist/composer, friend of Gabriel Fauré, who joined the artillery, August 1914.*

"Chanson De Guerre"

Dame Death is joyously dancing
a drunken, hip-swinging jig,
never a word, just wriggling
and playfully juggling skulls
like so many knucklebones.

Dame Death is glad, and very drunk -
for there's blood in full flow out there,
a heavy red brookful in every ravine.

Accompanying her weird dancing
is the tom-tom of guns in the distance:
"Tom-tom-tom! tom-tom-tom! Come then,
White Lady, come dance to the sound of the drums!"

Dame Death's getting drunker and splashing
her sweet little face with blood,
like a child who's been eating the jam.

Dame death is paddling in blood,
and slapping down into it with her long hands,
as though she were washing her shroud;
wallowing, and silently sniggering,
Dame Death is flushed, writhing, dancing
like a girl who's had too much to drink.

"Hey, Death, get your hopping in time
with the tom-tom of guns in the distance!"

- Tomtomtom-tomtomtom!
                The guns in the distance
quicken their murderous presto,
guns laughing together in rhythm;
the guns in the band force the tempo,
whipping her up for The Jubilation Ball:

"Spin on those dainty thin heels,
squirm the meat off those sinuous hips
get waltzing and whirling, White Lady!
dancing and skipping! waving your arms!

Here's blood, here's blood!
And here's some more, to keep you busy!
Come on now, drink up! totter and reel!
This is the start of the Orgy in Red!"

Dame Death is dancing, insanely drunk,
to the tom-tom of guns in the distance.

1916 he volunteered to fly as an observer of enemy artillery, but was shot down and died, 17 August 1917, near Verdun.

"La Fièvre" 1916, by Albert-Paul Granier

"Heartbeat, heartbeat, why the rush?
Whither the headlong dash,
where are you taking me,
where is this punishing mad gallop
dragging my dishevelled life?"

My heart is racing off, up through the clouds,
over the mountains, across the plains -
not Pécopin himself, on Satan's thoroughbred,
flew as swift through all those haunted years
as me, on this runaway heart
careering like a wild stallion.

"Where are you rushing me heart?"
"To a white hospital, in a quiet garden,
women softly rustling through the wards,
and, at nightfall, distant tranquil bells
murmuring a call to evensong;
to a white hospital, and a peaceful death,
a woman's white hand on your pale brow,

and precious words of comfort on her lips."
"No, rampaging heart! No!"
"Fetch my horse!"
- Sooner the fierce alarm-cry of guns
announcing torrents of thunder-strikes;
and sooner than the nurses' soft footsteps,
give me merciless flying splintered steel
whizzing invisible just above our heads!

No, heart...
Let me die beside rearing guns,
in the mad triumph of this great Epic,
die lying here, in the mud and the blood,
my eyes filled with sky, my heart with stars,
here, soothed by the moon's affectionate caress,
with a great chunk of steel in my chest!
A P Granier

Written at the front before he was killed at Verdun:

"**Le Pourquoi**" by Marc de Larreguy de Civrieux
"**Sans en comprendre le pourquoi**"

After the Charleroi affair
And since we waved the Marne goodbye,
I drag my carcass everywhere,
But never know the reason why.

In trench or barn I spend each day,
From fort or attic glimpse the sky,
At this war simply slog away,
But never know the reason why.

I ask, hoping to understand
This slaughter's purpose. The reply
I get is: "For the Motherland!"
But never know the reason why.

Better for me to just keep mum
And when it's my own turn to die,
Depart this life for kingdom come
But never know the reason why.
M de Civrieux - February 1916

Gaston De Ruyter Dim cho Debelyanov - a Bulgarian Symbolist

Debelyanov fought in the first Balkan War, 1912; later k.i.a. October 1916, in northern Macedonia, by Irish troops.

"A Hero's Dream"

The enemy's retreated and the noise
and smoke of battle's drifted over the hill.
Sleep and relief descend on weary eyes
and now once more the battlefield lies still.

And he, too, shuts his eyes and falls asleep,
his rifle butt supporting head and limb,
and thinks he hears his mother in the deep
enfolding silence whispering to him:

- Fear not the foe, my son, fear not his challenge,
even though in battle you may soon be killed:
your native land expects you to avenge
five hundred years of blood guiltlessly spilled.

If you're to die, die like a man, my son;
if you return, then know that the whole nation
will honour you for all that you have done,
staking your young life without hesitation.

Then she fell silent. He reached out and tried
to embrace her - then he saw, as he was waking,
the morning star still hanging in the sky
as on the horizon the new day was breaking.
The trumpets sounded the alarm. And while
fighting the battle with disdain of death
he fell, on his young lips a quiet smile:
a gallant hero to his final breath.

"To My Sons" - Poland, by J Zulawski

I went to the battle dear sons of mine
Like my father went and his father went
And his father's father, the world content
To cross with the legions hoping in time
Through the blood and the wounds a path he'd see
To a Poland that's ours a Poland that's free
Let's pray to God, dear sons of mine,
That the shackles binding our legs disappear,
And before you reach your grandfather's years
His dream of waking truth will incline
And the ages of blood which nourished the leas
Will make them blossom in a Poland that's free.
But if the good Lord dear sons of mine
Has not let the dew come from blood that we spilled
Then your hearts contain enough blood still
To give holy Freedom a new harvest time
And you will go your birthright's trustees
To fight for a Poland that's ours that is free.
J Zulawski

Josef Rust fought in Russia, 24 August 1915, at Orla, & wrote this song about that battle two months later, in Cambrai. His friend Ernst Brockman composed the melody there, on 20 April 1916, 11 weeks before he was killed at Verdun. Josef survived the war, just, badly wounded against France in 1918, and became a teacher and writer.

"Soon, all too soon (Bald Allzubalde)"

Alone in the woods, a flower blooms red
Soon all too soon, I too will be dead.
Flying somewhere is a small piece of lead
Coming to take away all my care
Today or tomorrow, all is the same.

Far down in the valley three spades are digging
A stone-cold grave for a soldier who's gone.
In the distance of twilight lies a small town
Where a young girl weeps in her lonely room,
Alone in the woods a flower blooms red
Soon all too soon, I too will be dead.
—music by Ernst Brockmann,
lyrics by Josef Rust

Capt. J E Crombie, son and grandson of MPs, commissioned at 18, on leaving Winchester College; to France February 1915, wounded in April — major operations in England. Returned to France, Cpt. Crombie's last poem, written in the village of Bray, a few miles NW of Arras, 8 April 1917, two weeks before he was killed at Bullecourt, near Arras, aged 20:

"Easter Day, 1917 - The Eve Of The Battle"

I rose and watched the eternal giant of fire
Renew his struggle with the grey monk Dawn,
Slowly supreme, though broadening streaks of blood
Besmirch the threadbare cloak, and pour his flood
Of life and strength on our yet sleeping choir,
As I went out to church on Easter morn.

Returning with the song of birds and men
Acclaiming victory of throbbing life,
I saw the fairies of the morning shower
Giving to drink each waking blade and flower,
I saw the new world take Communion then -
And now 'tis night and we return to strife.

J E Crombie

As with Wilfred Owen and many other war poets, much of Sassoon's poetry was imbued with Christian symbolism, and the trauma of trying to reconcile their Faith with their trench warfare experiences. So, three poems for Good Friday and Easter. The first two poems are by Siegfried Sassoon:

[Good Friday]

"Christ And The Soldier"

The straggled soldier halted - stared at Him -
Then clumsily dumped down upon his knees,
Gasping, 'O blessed crucifix, I'm beat!'
And Christ, still sentried by the seraphim,
Near the front-line, between two splintered trees,
Spoke him: 'My son, behold these hands and feet.'
The soldier eyed Him upward, limb by limb,
Paused at the Face; then muttered, 'Wounds like these
Would shift a bloke to Blighty just a treat!'
Christ, gazing downward, grieving and ungrim,
Whispered, 'I made for you the mysteries,
Beyond all battles moves the Paraclete.'

Siegfried Sassoon

Siegfried Sassoon's 1st front-line poem:

"The Redeemer"

He faced me, reeling in his weariness
Shouldering his load of planks, so hard to bear.
I say that He was Christ, who wrought to bless
All groping things with freedom bright as air
And with his mercy washed and made them fair.
Then the flame sank, and all grew black as pitch,
While we began to struggle along the ditch;
And someone flung his burden in the muck,
Mumbling: 'O Christ Almighty, now I'm stuck!'

[Easter Day] - Wilfred Owen rejects the hope of Resurrection, in words which his mother famously reversed on his grave-stone's epitaph, by omitting his second question mark.

"The End"

After the blast of lightning from the east,
  The flourish of loud clouds, the Chariot Throne,
After the drums of time have rolled and ceased,
  And by the bronze west long retreat is blown,
Shall Life renew these bodies? Of a truth,
  All death will he annul, all tears assuage?
And fill these void veins full again with youth,
  And wash, with an immortal water, age?

When I do ask white Age, he saith not so:
  'My head hangs weighed with snow.'
And when I hearken to the Earth, she saith:
  'My fiery heart shrinks, aching. It is death.
Mine ancient scars shall not be glorified,
Nor my titanic tears, the seas, be dried.

Van Beek, a South African, came to Britain in 1908 to attend Edinburgh university, and joined the Royal Field Artillery in 1914. He wrote this poem after being present at the first day of The Somme, but because of its anti-war outlook it was not published until 1919. Earlier, when he recited his war poems in London, he was severely reprimanded.

"After The Offensive"

This is the end of it, this the cold silence
Succeeding the violence
That rioted here.
This is the end of it – grim and austere.
This is the end of it – where the tide spread,
Runnels of blood
Debris of dead;
This is the end of it: ebb follows flood.
Waves of strong men
That will surge not again,
Scattered and riven
You lie, and you rot;
What have you not given?
And what – have you got?

Cyril Winterbotham was a lawyer called to the bar in 1911 and a Parliamentary candidate. Commissioned in the Glosters in 1914, on the Somme for 18 months, then to Arras in August 1916 by Ovillers-la-Boiselle; killed leading an attack at Ovillers, 27 August 1916, a month after writing this poem:

"The Cross Of Wood"

God be with you and us who go our way
And leave you dead upon the ground you won;
For you at last the long fatigue is done,
The hard march ended, you have rest today.
You were our friends, with you we watched the dawn
Gleam through the rain of the long winter night,
With you we laboured till the morning light
Broke on the village, shell-destroyed and torn.
Not now for you the glorious return
To steep Stroud valleys, to the Severn leas
By Tewksbury and Gloucester, or the trees
Of Cheltenham under high Cotswold stern.
For you no medals such as others wear -
A cross of bronze for those approved brave -
To you is given, above a shallow grave,
The Wooden Cross that marks you resting there.

Rest you content, more honourable far
Than all the Orders is the Cross of Wood,
The symbol of self-sacrifice that stood
Bearing the God whose brethren you are.

Lt. Cyril Winterbotham

A WOA scoop! Our thanks to Tim Steward, whose father Vernon, a New Zealand volunteer in the Boer War, wrote this poem, never before published, but hand-copied by his wife.

"**The Lonely Laager**" by V W W Steward

On the silent hills of Bothasberg
  Where the rank tambootie waves
There lies midst rocks and doings
  A lonely laager of graves.

It is pitched on the wind-swept ridges
  Of a kopje bleak and bare,
A common coign of vantage
  Which victor and vanquished share.

For there in that lonely sepulchre
  Both victor and vanquished lie; -
The battle's past, the strife is o'er
  For those who fought to die.

And there shall no drum-beat waken
  Nor bugle summon the line,
And there is no need for outposts
  Nor word for the countersign.

And nought but the stars keep vigil
  Over that lonesome camp,
Nought but the tambootie whispers
  In the night dews chill and damp.

And that silent host lies sleeping
  Side by side neath the mother sod
'Til they rise to the last loud challenge -
  The great roll call of God.

Geoffrey Kennedy, one of 3000 priests who accompanied the troops; he saved wounded men from No Man's Land at Messines, 1917, and won the MC. Later famous as "Woodbine Willy". Published pacifist essays, The Hardest Part, in 1919.

"Solomon In All His Glory"

Still I see them coming, coming,
 In their ragged broken line,
Walking wounded in the sunlight,
 Clothed in majesty divine.

For the fairest of the lilies,
 That God's summer ever sees,
Ne'er was clothed in royal beauty
 Such as decks the least of these.

Tattered, torn, and bloody khaki,
 Gleams of white flesh in the sun,
Raiment worthy of their beauty,
 And the great things they have done.

Purple robes and snowy linen
 Have for earthly kings sufficed,
But these bloody sweaty tatters
 Were the robes of Jesus Christ.

Geoffrey Kennedy

At 45 when war broke out, poet Laurence Binyon was too old to enlist, so volunteered for British military hospitals in France in 1915, and again to rescue wounded from the battle of Verdun in 1916. He is most famous for his "For The Fallen", recited at Remembrance festivals every year; and he composed "The Burning of the Leaves" for the Second World War.

"The Arras Road"

I

The early night falls on the plain
In cloud and desolating rain.
I see no more, but feel around
The ruined earth, the wounded ground.

There in the dark, on either side
The road, are all the brave who died.
I think not on the battles won;
I think on those whose day is done.

Heaped mud, blear pools, old rusted wire,
Cover their youth and young desire.
Near me they sleep, and they to me
Are dearer than their victory.

II

Where now are they who once had peace
Here, and the fruitful tilth's increase?
Shattered is all their hands had made,
And the orchards where their children played.

But night, that brings the darkness, brings
The heart back to its dearest things.
I feel old footsteps plodding slow
On ways that they were used to know.

And from my own land, past the strait,
From homes that no more news await,
Absenting thoughts come hither flying
To the unknown earth where Love is lying.

There are no stars to-night, but who
Knows what far eyes of lovers true
In star-like vigil, each alone
Are watching now above their own?

III

England and France unconscious tryst
Keep in this void of shadowy mist
By phantom Vimy, and mound that tell
Of ghostliness that was Gravelle.

The rain comes wildly down to drench
Disfeatured ridge, deserted trench.
Guns in the night, far, far away
Thud on the front beyond Cambrai.

But here the night is holy, and here
I will remember, and draw near,
And for a space, till night be sped,
Be with the beauty of the dead.

Laurence Binyon

"Last Song"

All my songs are risen and fled away;
(Only the brave birds stay);
All my beautiful songs are broken or fled.
My poor songs could not stay
Among the filth and the weariness and the dead.
There was bloody grime on their light, white feathery wings,
(Hear how the lark still sings),
And their eyes were the eyes of dead men that I knew.
Only a madman sings
When half of his friends lie asleep for the rain and the dew.
The flowers will grow over the bones of my friends;
(The birds' song never ends);
Winter and summer, their fair flesh turns to clay.
Perhaps before all ends
My songs will come again that have fled away.

Henry Lamont Simpson

Lt. Henry Simpson, *wounded at Ypres Aug.1917, evacuated to Winchester then home to Carlisle...*

"Last Nocturne"

The search-light swords
Stab the sky
Miles back,
Light taut cords
Of gold, high
Against the black.

A star-flare
Of showering red
Surprises the night,
And hangs in the air,
Painting the dead
With ruddy light.

The pale wax
Of their faces
Turns to blood
By dim tracks
In dark places
Of the wood

Where I go
Hurrying on.
Suddenly
I stumble low
On some one.
God on high!

His face was very cold,
And very white;
There was no blood.
I grew old
That night
In the wood.

He was young,
My enemy -
But lips the same
As lips have sung
Often with me.
I whispered the name

Of the friend whose face
Was so like his;
But never a sound
In the dim place
Under the trees
Closing around.

Then I cursed
My Nocturnes -
I hated night;
Hated it worst
When the moon turns
Her tired light

On horrible things
Man has done
With life and love.
Only a fool sings
When night's begun
And the moon's above.

I cursed each song
I made for men
Full of moonlight

Lasting night-long;
For I knew then
How evil is night.

I cursed each tune
Of night-dim wood
And Naiad's stream,
By that mad moon
A search for blood
And the waxen gleam

Of dead faces
Under the trees
In the trampled grass,
Till the bloody traces
Of the agonies
Of night-time pass.

Henry L Simpson

Back from his convalescence near Winchester and at home, Henry Simpson was sniped reconnoitring No Man's Land near Hazebrouck, 29 August 1918, aged 21. This was his last poem, untitled, alas prophetic: - 'he died young'.

If it should chance that I be cleansed and crowned
With sacrifice and agony and blood,
And reach the quiet haven of Death's arms,
Nobly companioned of that brotherhood
Of common men who died and laughed the while,
And so made shine a flame that cannot die,
But flares a glorious beacon down the years -
If it should happen thus some one may come
And pouring over dusty lists may light
Upon my long-forgotten name and musing
May say a little sadly - even now
Almost forgetting why he should be sad -
May say 'And he died young' and then forget...

H L S

Cpt. Vivian Pemberton MC, Royal Garrison Artillery 1914-18. Eldest brother Oswald was killed in 1914, twin brother Alexander fought at Gallipoli and survived the war. Vivian k.i.a. at Sancourt, 7 October 1918.

"An Only Son's Dying Lament"

I'm not a soldier born and bred,
I hate the sound of guns,
I joined because they told me
England needed all her sons.

I love old England's country scenes,
The old cliffs by the sea,
The peaceful, mist-clad Devon moors,
'Tis there that I would be.

I love the gentle English girls,
I love their graceful ways,
I love to watch the sheep dog's work,
And the lazy cattle graze.

They use to give me all I asked
In those dear days of old,
They gave me wine, they gave me love,
And never asked for gold.

But now I do not ask for love,
For riches, wine, or song,
They tell me that I'll soon be well,
But I know they are wrong.

A stretcher party brought me here,
My left leg hurt like sin,
They sent my pay-book and my gold
Back to my next of kin.
It is not much for which I ask,
I know my knell has rung,
But they will not give me anything
To cool my burning tongue.

Vivian Pemberton MC

Max Plowman was born in London, worked in his father's brick works, then became a journalist. A conscientious objector, he nevertheless joined the RAMC Ambulance service, then took a commission. Concussed by a shell on the Somme, he was treated by Dr Rivers at Craiglockhart. In 1918 he was court-martialled for his principles, and dismissed from the army...

"**The Dead Soldiers**" by Max Plowman

I

Spectrum Trench. Autumn. Nineteen-Sixteen.
And Zenith. (The Border Regiment will remember.)
A little north of where Lesboeufs had been.
(The Australians took it over in December.)
Just as the scythe had caught them, there they lay,
A sheaf for Death, ungarnered and untied:
A crescent moon of men who showed the way
When first the Tanks crept out, till they too died:
Guardsmen, I think, but one could hardly tell,
It was a forward slope, beyond the crest,
Muddier than any place in Dante's hell,
Where sniping gave us very little rest.
At night one stumbled over them and swore;
Each day the rain hid them a little more.

II

Fantastic forms, in posturing attitudes,
Twisted or bent, or lying deathly prone;
Their individual hopes my thought eludes,
But each man had a hope to call his own.
Much else? — God knows. But not for me the thought,
'Your mothers made your bodies: God your souls,
And, for because you dutifully fought,
God will go mad and make of half-lives, wholes.'
No. God in every one of you was slain;
For killing men is always killing God,
Though life destroyed shall come to life again
And loveliness rise from the sodden sod.
But if of life we do destroy the best,
God wanders wide, and weeps in his unrest.

CSM W H Littlejohn, k.i.a. at Arras, 10 April 1917

"**A Prayer**" by W H Littlejohn

Lord, if it be Thy will
That I enter the great shadowed valley that lies
Silent, just over the hill,
Grant, they may say, "There's a comrade that dies

Waving his hand to us still!"
Lord, if there come the end,
Let me find space and breath all the dearest I prize
Into Thy hands to commend:
Then let me go, with my boy's laughing eyes
Smiling a word to a friend.

"A Soldier" by T P Cameron Wilson

He laughed. His blue eyes searched the morning
Found the unceasing song of the lark
In a brown twinkle of wings, far out.
Great clouds, like galleons, sailed the distance.
The young spring day had slipped the cloak of dark
And stood up straight and naked with a shout.

Through the green wheat, like laughing schoolboys,
Tumbled the yellow mustard flowers, uncheck'd.
The wet earth reeked and smoked in the sun...
He thought of the waking farm in England
The deep thatch of the roof — all shadow-fleck'd
The clank of pails at the pump... the day begun.
"After the war..." he thought. His heart beat faster
With a new love for things familiar and plain.
The Spring leaned down and whispered to him low
Of a slim, brown-throated woman he had kissed...
He saw, in sons that were himself again,
The only immortality that man may know.

And then a sound grew out of the morning,
And a shell came, moving a destined way,
Thin and swift and lustful, making its moan.
A moment his brave white body knew the Spring,
The next, it lay
In a red ruin of blood and guts and bone.
Oh! Nothing was tortured there! Nothing could know
How Death blasphemed all men and their high birth
With his obscenities. Already moved,
Within those shattered tissues, that dim force,
Which is the ancient alchemy of Earth,
Changing him to the very flowers he loved.
"Nothing was tortured there!" Oh, pretty thought!
When God Himself might well bow down His head
And hide His haunted eyes before the dead.

"**This Generation**" by Osbert Sitwell

Already a serving officer in the Grenadier Guards, Osbert Sitwell was sent to Ypres in 1914, where he began to write poetry, leaving the army in 1918 as a Captain.

Their youth was fevered - passionate, quick to drain
  The last few pleasures from the cup of life
Before they turned to suck the dregs of pain
  And end their young-old lives in mortal strife.
They paid the debts of many a hundred year
  Of foolishness and riches in alloy.
They went to death; nor did they shed a tear
  For all they sacrificed of love and joy.
Their tears ran dry when they were in the womb,
For, entering life - they found it was their tomb.

"**Jo's Requiem**" by Ernest Rhys

He had the ploughman's strength
in the grasp of his hand:
He could see a crow
three miles away,
and the trout beneath a stone.
He could hear the green oats growing,
and the south-west wind making rain.
He could hear the wheel upon the hill
when it left the level road.
He could make a gate, and dig a pit,
and plough as straight as stone can fall.
And he is dead.

Like Henry Simpson, Digby Bertram Haseler deferred his place to read History at Cambridge and enlisted in the Shropshire Infantry on leaving Hereford Cathedral School, sending this poem to his college magazine:

"**At A British Cemetery In Flanders**"

Here lie no mercenaries who, for gold
  Bartered their strength and skill and their life's blood;
These men led homely lives, and looked to grow old
  In peace earning a quiet livelihood.
Yet when the drums made summons near and far
  They sprang to arms, pitifully unprepared
For the great agony of modern war;
  And here in Flanders with their comrades shared

Honour and pain, and here in Flanders died
  Unflinching ... Weep a little and be content,
Strong in your faith and in your measureless pride,
  Their trial was great and their death excellent.

As W N Hodgson's poem "Ave, Mater - atque Vale" used a popular Latin tag, so Haseler's poem is peppered with allusions, not only to Horace but to Brooke's sonnet (the "must" is more pessimistic than "should") and the famous "Barrage lifts" toast given by Gordon Haswell. As senior Captain of the 9th Battalion, Kings Own Yorkshire Light Regiment, Haswell was obliged, on the spur of the moment, at officers' drinks 29th June, just before the 1st July 1916 attack on Fricourt, where the battalion was reduced from 800 to 80 men, Haswell among the fallen.

"Stray Leaves" by Digby B Haseler

As I tramped off to join the fight
  A blackbird nodded to me — so!
Said, 'Hope we'll see you back all right.
  Keep safe. Cheero!'
We carried all before us in the attack,
Broke through their lines and captured all the town -
A splendid victory! But we buried Jack
At Dead Man's Corner when the sun went down.

For my first night in a strange bed
I toss and turn and restless lie,
While cruel dreams chase through my head
And hideous forms go laughing by.
Tell me, brothers, how shall I fare
When the good body strong and brave
Sleeps with Death, and cold and bare
I spend my first night in the grave?

If I must die write not, " 'Tis sweet
  To fall for England in the fray."
But write, "Non omnis periit.
  Sed miles, sed pro patria."
And add this one short line that fits -
"Gentlemen, when the barrage lifts ... "

For O, it must be hard to die
  And leave the best of life behind
To lie beneath an alien sky
  Unknown, untended, hard to find.
To leave earth's red and green and gold
And turn to a little bitter mould.

Joining the Scots Guards when he left Eton in 1916, Perowne served for the war then became a career diplomat.

"A Dirge"

Thou art no longer here,
No longer shall we see thy face,
But, in that other place,
Where may be heard
The roar of the world rushing down the wantways of the stars;
And the silver bars
Of heaven's gate
Shine soft and clear:
Thou mayest wait.

No longer shall we see
Thee walking in the crowded streets,
But where the ocean of the Future beats
Against the flood-gates of the Present, swirling to this earth,
Another birth
Thou mayest have;
Another Arcady
May thee receive.
Not here thou dost remain,
Thou art gone far away,
Where, at the portals of the day,
The hours ever dance in ring, a silvern-footed throng,

While Time looks on,
And seraphs stand
Choiring an endless strain
On either hand.

Thou canst return no more;
Not as the happy time of spring
Comes after winter burgeoning
On wood and wold in folds of living green, for thou art dead.
Our tears we shed
In vain, for thou
Dost pace another shore,
Untroubled now.

Victor Perowne

Three poems by W N Hodgson MC, son of the Archdeacon of Lindisfarne, scholar at Durham School, here referenced - the first from August 1915, shortly before he won the MC at Loos, the second from 8 June 1916, near Mametz, where he is buried in the Devonshire Cemetery at Mansel Copse.

"Reverie"

At home they see on Skiddaw
His royal purple lie
And Autumn up in Newlands
Arrayed in russet die,
Or under burning woodland
The still lake's gramarye.
And far off and grim and sable
The menace of the Gable,
Lifts up his stark aloofness
Against the western sky.

At vesper-time in Durham
The level evening falls
Upon the shadowy river
That slides by ancient walls,
Where out of crannied turrets
The mellow belfry calls.
And there sleep brings forgetting
And morning no regretting,
And love is laughter-wedded
To health in happy halls.
But here are blood and blisters
And thirst as hard as sand
And interminable travelling
Interminable land;

And stench and filth and sickness
And hate by hardship fanned.
The haunt of desolation
Wherein a desperate nation
Writhes in the grip of murder's
Inexorable hand.

Above the graves of heroes
The wooden crosses grow,
That shall no more see Durham
Nor any place they know,
Where fell tops face the morning
And great winds blow;

Who loving as none other
The land that is their mother
Unfaltering renounced her
Because they loved her so.

"Durham Cathedral"

Above the storied city, ringed about
 With shining waters, stands God's ancient house,
Over the windy uplands gazing out
 Towards the sea, and deep about it drowse
The grey dreams of the buried centuries,
 And through all time across the rustling weirs
An ancient river passes; thus it lies,
 Exceeding wise and strong and full of years.
Often within those dreaming aisles we heard,
 Breaking the level flow of sombre chords,
A trumpet-call of melody that stirred
 The blood and pierced the heart like flaming swords.
Long years we learned and grew, and in this place
 Put on the harness of our manhood's state,
And then with fearless heart and forward face,
 Went strongly forth to try a fall with fate.
And so we passed and others had our room,
 But well we know that here till days shall cease,
While the great stream goes seaward and trees bloom,
 God's kindness dwells about these courts of peace.

W N Hodgson MC

Hodgson dedicates his life to his 'Alma Mater', across the river Wear from the Castle and Cathedral, high on their promontory:

"Ave, Mater - atque Vale"

The deathless mother, grey and battle-scarred,
Lies in the sanctuary of stately trees,
Where the deep Northern night is saffron starred
Above her head, and thro' the dusk she sees
God's shadowy fortress keep unsleeping guard.
From her full breast we drank of joy and mirth
And gave to her a boy's unreasoned heart,
Wherein Time's fullness was to bring to birth
Such passionate allegiance that to part

Seemed like the passing of all light on earth.
Now on the threshold of a man's estate,
With a new depth of love akin to pain
I ask thy blessing, while I dedicate
My life and sword, with promise to maintain
Thine ancient honour yet inviolate.
Last night dream-hearted in the Abbey's spell
We stood to sing old Simeon's passing hymn,
When sudden splendour of the sunset fell
Full on my eyes, and passed and left all dim -
At once a summons and a deep farewell.
I am content - our life is but a trust
From the great hand of God, and if I keep
The immortal Treasure clean of mortal rust
Against His claim, 'tis well and let me sleep
Among the not dishonourable dust.

W N Hodgson MC

Francis Ledwidge enlisted in October 1914, an Irish private, and fought in the Dardanelles and Bulgaria. Wounded in Bulgaria, he was in hospital in Cairo for 4 months, then shipped to hospital in Manchester, April 1916.

"Ascension Day, 1917"

Lord, Thou hast left Thy footprints in the rocks,
That we may know the way to follow Thee,
But there are wide lands opened out between
Thy Olivet and my Gethsemane.

And often times I make the night afraid,
Crying for lost hands when the dark is deep
And strive to reach the sheltering of Thy love
Where Thou are herd among Thy folded sheep.

Thou wilt not ever thus, O Lord, allow
My feet to wander when the sun is set,
But through the darkness, let me still behold
The stoney bye-ways up to Olivet.

Francis Ledwidge

Later, in 1917, Ledwidge was posted to Belgium.

"A Soldier's Grave"

Then in the lull of midnight, gentle arms
Lifted him slowly down the slopes of death,
Lest he should hear again the mad alarms
Of battle, dying moans, and painful breath.

And where the earth was soft for flowers we made
A grave for him that he might better rest.
So, Spring shall come and leave it sweet arrayed,
And there the lark shall turn her dewy nest.

"Soliloquy"

When I was young I had a care
Lest I should cheat me of my share
Of that which makes it sweet to strive
For life, and dying still survive,
A name in sunshine written higher
Than lark or poet dare aspire.
I was so very bad the neighbours
Spoke of me at their daily labours.

And now I'm drinking wine in France,
The helpless child of circumstance.
To-morrow will be loud with war,
How will I be accounted for?
It is too late now to retrieve
A fallen dream, too late to grieve
A name unmade, but not too late
To thank the gods for what is great;
A keen-edged sword, a soldier's heart,
Is greater than a poet's art.
And greater than a poet's fame
A little grave that has no name.
Whence honour turns away in shame.

Francis Ledwidge

Ledwidge was k.i.a. at Pilckem, with fellow poets J Hobson & E Evans - known as "Hedd Wyn" - 31 July 1917, 1st day, 3rd Battle of Ypres, at Passchendaele, three of the 31,000 killed that day; they are buried together in Artillery Wood cemetery.

"**War**" by Hedd Wyn (E Evans)

Bitter to live in times like these.
While God declines beyond the seas;
Instead, man, king or peasantry,
Raises his gross authority.

When he thinks God has gone away
Man takes up his sword to slay
His brother; we can hear death's roar.
It shadows the hovels of the poor.

Like the old songs they left behind,
We hung our harps in the willows again.
Ballads of boys blow on the wind,
Their blood is mingled with the rain.

Alec de Candole, son of a priest and intending to follow his father into the Church, postponed his Cambridge scholarship and enlisted as soon as he left Marlborough in 1916. In Flanders, from April 1917, Alec de Candole is worshipping in a camp at Dickebusch, conflicted by the thought of Christ dying to save men, who now murder each other:

In that rough barn we knelt, and took and ate
Simply together there the bread divine,
The body of God made flesh, and drank the wine
His blood who died, to man self-dedicate.
And even while we knelt, a sound of hate
Burst sudden on us, as our shrieking line
Of guns flashed bursting death, a thunderous sign
Of raging evil in our human state.
Strange state! when good must use (nor other can)
The tools of ill, itself from ill to free,
And Christ must fight with Satan's armoury.
What strange and piteous contrast may we scan,
The shell that slays, and Christ upon the tree,
The love that died, and man that murders man!
June 1917

Candole considers the many casualties and clutches at hope, but, musing on his life so far, though only twenty years old, is also resigned to the worst, in a second untitled poem:

For them, the bitterness of death is past;
For us, we know not how our lot is cast,
To live or die, or worse, to suffer pain,
That rends and tears the body and soul atwain,
Until death come, a kindly friend, at last.

And stirrings deeper yet — I have loved the earth,
Known sorrow that enriched the after-mirth;
The past was good, the future bright; I burn
Still, still, to see the golden years return,
And plenty bear oblivion of our dearth.

But still, if hope, with each departing wing,
Should leave me starless, night-bound, sorrowing,
Yet fate, my master, bids me follow still,
Content, perchance: and if against my will,
I follow on, a bound and helpless thing.

Therefore I cling to hope: and yet my soul
Shall follow fate content whate'er the goal,
So free, though every lightsome hope be gone,
Can rest secure upon herself alone,
One small firm rock whatever surges roll.

Alec de Candole - June, 1917

Candole was wounded in Flanders, October 1917, convalesced in England, and composed two sonnets at Christmas - the first one bemoaning Man's folly:

I saw them laughing once; they held their sides
And laughed till old Olympus shook again, -
The blessed gods, who watch whate'er betides
On earth below, saw man with man in vain
Strive in besotted hate, crawl out at night
And creep about, and hide in fear the day,
Burrowing beneath the earth at dawn's first light,
And sleeping all the golden hours away
Of sun and pleasure; then when night grows chill,
Though bright the full moon shines upon the earth
He calls it dark, comes out, and works his will.
Small wonder surely for Olympus' mirth,
At war, sans right, sans reason, and sans mind.
This wild supremest folly of mankind!

In Salisbury cathedral Candole had prayed for God's protection before his first tour, and now he returns there to renew that plea before he is sent back out:

"Salisbury Cathedral"

I Prayed here when I faced the future first
Of war and death, that GOD would grant me power
To serve Him truly, and through best and worst
He would protect and guide me every hour.
And He has heard my prayer, and led me still
Through purging war's grim wondrous revelation
Of fear and courage, death and life, until
I kneel again in solemn adoration
Before Him here, and still black clouds before
Threat as did those which now passed through are bright;
Therefore, with hope and prayer and praise, once more
I worship Him, and ask that with His might
He still would lead, and I with utter faith
Follow, through life or sharpest pain or death.

Two more sonnets in praise of Candole's home country:

"England I"

I CANNOT argue out the rights and wrongs,
Who first this hideous force of war did move,
I only know my heart and spirit longs
To serve this England somehow which I love.
Shall it be ours to dwell where England's hills
Roll down in lonely places to the sea.
And hear the rushing waterfall that fills
The vale with music's deep profundity,
And shall not love compel us, whatsoe'er
This England asks, so beautiful, so great,
To do or suffer, and our end be there,
Not hating, though the foeman merit hate,
But simply glad to pay, if need, the price
Of so much beauty in life's sacrifice?

"England II"

Life thus, perchance, is short; but life is worth
More, if your home is England; twenty years
Of living in the loveliest land on earth
Are better than an age where Afric sears
The soul with summer's fires, or Arctic cold
Numbs dead the very brain with wintry stress.
Yes, England, though thou listen to the bold
And braggart cries of folly and shamelessness,
Flinging rewards to those who ask reward.
Thy true sons love thee yet, and loathe the brood
Of cursed traitors. Free thyself, and guard
Thy noble heart unchanged, and ancient blood;
Thee will we answer, not the blatant breath
Of knaves, but thy high call, to life or death.

Alec de Candole

Following his convalescence, Candole retrained for the Machine Gun Corps and returned to Ypres, July 1918:

"And If A Bullet"

And if a bullet in the midst of strife
Should still the pulse of this unique life,
'Twere well: be death an everlasting rest,
I oft could yearn for it, by cares opprest;
And be't a night that brings another day,
I still could go rejoicing on my way,
Desiring in no phantom heav'n to dwell,
Nor scared with terror of any phantom hell,
But gazing now I find not death a curse
Better than life perchance, at least not worse;
Only the fierce and rending agony,
The torment of the flesh about to die,
Affrights my soul; but that shall pass anon,
And death's repose or strife be found, that gone;
Only with that last earthly ill to cope
God grant me strength, and I go forth with hope.

A month later, August 23rd, now troubled by the 'Wild waste of war' and asking 'Why God...?' but still clinging to his faith, Candole wrote this sonnet:

"Hope"

O monstrous din of struggle purposeless,
Wild waste of war that means not anything,
Keen lead and whistling steel that burn and sting,
O riddle ever graver in its stress,
Unsolved enigma yet of wickedness ;
Why, if there is a God who is a King,
Can earth be made a hell in spite of spring,
And ravage soil the summer's flowery dress?
And yet, behind the strident howling blast,
The blinding lightning and the deaf'ning storm,
Still moves, I know, the one eternal Form,
The unity of all things, silent, vast,
And That shall yet restore creation's norm,
And clear all doubts, and heal all wounds, at last.

August 23rd, 1918.

Candole's final sonnet, composed a week later, is called 'Faith' — but he is sorely tried in justifying it:

"Faith"

Why do we madly rob ourselves in vain,
Cast life and treasure recklessly away,
And lose our richest in our zeal to slay,
Enlarging wickedness and kindling pain?
And only faith returns an answer plain:
That somehow, sometime yet shall dawn the day,
When gloom of night shall yield to twilight grey,
And twilight to full noon give place again.
But ask you, how I dare to hold confess'd
This faith, when all the world is harsh and stark,
And only evil all around I mark?
I answer: Either all is but a jest,
Wrought by a purposeless demon in the dark
(Which soul denies), or all is for the best.

September 1st, 1918.

Candole was killed during a bombing raid near Aubigny, north-west of Arras, 3 September. Shortly before participating in the Somme offensive, in which he was wounded, Vernède composed:

"A Petition"

All that a man might ask, thou hast given me, England,
Birthright and happy, childhood's long heart's-ease,
And love whose range is deep beyond all sounding
And wider than all seas.

A heart to front the world and find God in it,
Eyes blind enow, but not too blind to see
The lovely things behind the dross and darkness,
And lovelier things to be.

And friends whose loyalty time nor death shall weaken,
And quenchless hope and laughter's golden store;
All that a man might ask thou hast given me, England,
Yet grant thou one thing more:

That now when envious foes would spoil thy splendour,
Unversed in arms, a dreamer such as I
May in thy ranks be deemed not all unworthy,
England, for thee to die.

R E Vernède

Lt Col Frederick Bendall, after six months' convalescence in Britain, was posted to the Somme, July 1916, near Ginchy.

"To G.S.B. (Blagbrough)"

Major Blagbrough, a school-master, Bendall's best friend, was commissioned September 1914 and fought on the Somme, where he was Killed in Action, 11 December 1916.

In peace they said "prepare for war" my friend
So you and I in those far happy days
Began in sport - but for a serious end
Our mimic warfare and our martial ways.
And when, at night, beside our mutual fire
We made and unmade kings, and tore the skies
Apart to read the future, you - desire
The father of your thought - with savant eyes
Saw the Red Cloud that swallowed us and said
That this would come which has come, and were glad -
Were glad altho' you saw the cloud blood red;

And I - I laughed, and said that you were mad.
So. It has come. Your dreams were all too true.
I have played many games with you. They are done.
But this I know, and knowing smile - that you
Have played the greatest game of all - and won.
So fare you well, my friend. Indeed I know
That you fare well. It must be thus - for He
Who died to make men good will have it so
For all of those who died to make men free.

by F W D Bendall

Lt. John Louis-Crommelin Brown MC who was educated at Winchester and Cambridge, was a first class batsman and Repton schoolmaster, and had an even busier war than A P Herbert and Henry Simpson, serving 3 years and 8 months, first in the Royal Scots, at Ypres for 3 months, until wounded in May 1915; then joining the Seaforth Highlanders in 1916, at Vimy Ridge. Posted to Fricourt and Mametz in July; then sent home with trench fever.
Back again in January 1917, to Blagny, Arras; wounded in the April battle, and won the MC; again sent home to recover. 1918, to Belgium, 11 April, shot near Wytschaete.

Four short, early poems, all untitled:

A verse of an early poem, written at Balliol, 1911:

And thus the music of Achilles' life
Burst from its prison, singing its sweet song
Unheard but by the soul. Meanwhile the strife
Of war rekindled round him; but its sound
Sung him that love in life was ne'er so strong
As love that passed, at death, laughing beneath the ground.

John Brown - Written at Ypres, April 1915:

Ye seeds of sorrow that lie hidden deep
In darkness 'neath the earth of my sad heart,
Why does not life within your hard husks leap?
Why do ye lie so cold and still apart?

Fear not that when ye shoot into the light
I'll tear ye up ere ye have time to flower,
For I will tend and keep ye free from blight,
And warm you with my smiles; till one soft hour

Will see your buds break into flowers of mirth,
Tossing before the dancing April wind,

That blows over my soul's fresh turned earth,
While pleasant Spring encompasseth my mind.

John Brown - Written in Leicester hospital, Summer 1915:

Arise, my heart, and dance,
And laugh, my soul!
The sun may look askance,
And o'er the sky clouds roll.

If a man's own soul is cold,
No July sun can warm;
If joy a man's heart hold
No winter blast can harm.

So walk the world with a springing pace,
Breathe in the whistling wind,
Till the red blood runs its riot race,
And warms the ice-bound mind.

John Brown, written when invalided home with trench fever, Summer 1916:

For weeks the rains of sorrow have soaked
The wood in my heart's cold hearth;
And the windows and doors of my soul are choked,
And the sunbeams can find no path.

And half-burnt matches are strewn around,
That flamed and could not light
The fire that I laid with care on the ground
To warm life and make it bright.

The sun of love alone can dry
The sticks that will not burn:
No patent match that wealth can buy
Will give the light I yearn.

So I sit and shiver and wait for Spring,
While sad-voiced winds still roar,
Till April in her hands shall bring
Love's first beams to my door.

J Brown

W N Ewer, journalist, conscientious objector, pacifist and communist; this poem published as early as 3 October 1914:

"Five Souls"

First Soul
I was a peasant of the Polish plain;
I left my plough because the message ran:-
Russia, in danger, needed every man
To save her from the Teuton; and was slain.
I gave my life for freedom - This I know
For those who bade me fight had told me so.

Second Soul
I was a Tyrolese, a mountaineer;
I gladly left my mountain home to fight
Against the brutal treacherous Muscovite;
And died in Poland on a Cossack spear.
I gave my life for freedom - This I know
For those who bade me fight had told me so.

Third Soul
I worked in Lyons at my weaver's loom,
When suddenly the Prussian despot hurled
His felon blow at France and at the world;
Then I went forth to Belgium and my doom.
I gave my life for freedom - This I know
For those who bade me fight had told me so.

Fourth Soul
I owned a vineyard by the wooded Main,
Until the Fatherland, begirt by foes
Lusting her downfall, called me, and I rose
Swift to the call - and died in far Lorraine.
I gave my life for freedom - This I know
For those who bade me fight had told me so.

Fifth Soul
I worked in a great shipyard by the Clyde;
There came a sudden word of wars declared,
Of Belgium, peaceful, helpless, unprepared,
Asking our aid: I joined the ranks, and died.
I gave my life for freedom - This I know
For those who bade me fight had told me so.

W N Ewer

Lt. A J Mann, Black Watch, posted to the Somme, August 1916, where he composed these two poems:

"The Soldier"

'Tis strange to look on a man that is dead
As he lies in the shell-swept hell,
And to think that the poor black battered corpse
Once lived like you and was well.

'Tis stranger far when you come to think
That you may be soon like him ...
And it's Fear that tugs at your trembling soul,
A Fear that is weird and grim.

"Before"

At least say this: my mem'ry will be dear
With that sad sweetness which is nobly fine.
I ask no more: the rest cannot be changed;
Let memory and tenderness be mine.
And may I die more nobly than I live
(For I have lived in folly and regret):
Then in the last Great Moment when I pass,
I shall have paid my Life's outstanding Debt!

A J Mann

Two more poems by Lt. A J Mann, the first written near Albert, on his way to High Wood, 8 October 1916.

"The Zenith"

To-day I reach the zenith of my life!
No time more noble in my span of years
Than this, the glorious hour of splendid strife,
Of War, of cataclysmal woe, and tears.

Mann's last poem, composed three days before he was fatally wounded at the Battle of Arras, 9 April 1917:

"The Great Dead"

Some lie in graves beside the crowded dead
In village churchyards; others shell holes keep,
Their bodies gaping, all their splendour sped.
Peace, O my soul ... A Mother's part to weep.

Say: do they watch with keen all-seeing eyes
My own endeavours in the whirling hell?
Ah, God! how great, how grand the sacrifice.
Ah, God! the manhood of yon men who fell!

And this is war ... Blood and a woman's tears,
Brave memories adown the quaking years.

A J Mann

SCOTS & MUD

Ivor Gurney enthuses over his new friends in the trenches, at Christmas 1916.

"**Scots**" by Ivor Gurney 4 January 1917

The boys who laughed and jested with me but yesterday
So fit for kings to speak to, so blithe and proud and gay,
Are now thoughts of blind pain, and best hid away...
(Over the top this morning at the dawn's first gray.)

O if we catch the kaiser his dirty hide to flay,
We'll hang him on a tall tree his pride to allay;
That will not bring the boys again to mountain and brae...
(Over the top this morning at the dawn's first gray.)

To think - Earth's best and dearest turned to red broken clay
By one devil's second! What words can we say?
Or what gift has God their mothers' anguish to repay?...
(Over the top this morning at the first flush of day.)

My Dear Miss Scott 7 January 1917

... I have met some fine people, by God. It sometimes seems worth it all now, and after the war, it will have seemed supremely worth while. It will have given England another topic of conversation other than the weather!
One of my Scots Engineers recited To the Haggis, Tom O'Shanter, the Daisy; and sang Ae Waukin O and John Anderson, and McGregor's gathering very well.
And then on Hogmanay - New Year's Eve you know, the pipers up in the village burst out in welcome for the New Year with a glorious tune that set us all aching to dance. 'We've been happy a'thegither'. Over and over it went.

Ivor Gurney

the Ubiquitous MUD !

Gurney is already an expert on MUD - "But O, the mud!"
(It was universally acknowledged that the Winter of 1916-1917 was the coldest, harshest weather ever experienced)

9 December 1916 "...now that the land is a sea of mud, and thoughts as grey as the weather... it is better to live a grey life in mud and danger, so long as one uses it as a means to an end." Ivor Gurney

22 December 1916 ..."today my batt: goes into the line, to stand in frozen mud to the knees; to live 15 hours in the dark every 24 hours. I spend 8 hours a day tramping about in mud and half-frozen water."

Ivor Gurney

Sidney Rogerson - November 1916

"I had not gone twenty yards before I encountered the MUD, mud unique even for the Somme, like walking through caramel. At every step the foot stuck fast, only wrenched out by a determined effort, bringing pounds of earth till legs ached in every muscle. No one could struggle through that mud for more than a few yards without rest. Terrible in its clinging consistency, it was the arbiter of destiny, the supreme enemy, paralysing and mocking English and German alike. Distances were measured not in yards but in mud."

17 January 1917 "Artillery horses, flogged so often out of the mud, have at last stuck there through weakness and been shot to save trouble."

Ivor Gurney

4 January 1917 Wilfred Owen meets MUD: "After those two days, we were let down, gently, into the real thing, Mud. It has penetrated now into that Sanctuary my sleeping bag, and that holy of holies my pyjamas." (to his mother Susan)

16 January 1917 "It was of course dark, and the ground was not mud, not sloppy mud, but an octopus of sucking clay, 3, 4, and 5 feet deep, relieved only by craters full of water. Men have been known to drown in them. Many stuck in the mud & and only got on by leaving their waders, equipment, and in some cases their clothes."

Wilfred Owen

Wilfred Owen's poems, composed winter 1917-18:
"I, too, saw God through mud - The mud that cracked on cheeks when wretches smiled"

Apologia.

"Tonight, this frost will fasten on this mud and us,"

Exposure.

" 'Till slowly lowered, his whole face kissed the mud."

The Last Laugh.

Sassoon's Diary: - MUD 29 November 1915

Went with working-party 3 o'clock. Wet day. Awful mud up in trenches. Tried to dig until 7.30 and came home soaked, 9.45. A shocking night for the men, whose billets are wretched.

"We lugged our clay-sucked boots as best we might"

- The Redeemer

12 April 1917 - The snow has gone and left bad mud... One of our tanks stuck in the mud getting over the trench - very wide... Rained all day - trenches like glue...

16 April 1917 - I got a sniper's bullet through the shoulder... got wound seen to at Aid Post in (Hindenburg) tunnel, walked to Hénin, told to walk on to Boyelles. Got there very beat, having foot-slogged four kilometres through mud. S.S.

"The Song of the MUD" by Mary Borden

This is the song of the mud
The pale yellow glistening mud that covers the hills like satin;
The grey gleaming silvery mud that is spread like enamel over the valleys;
The frothing, squirting spurting liquid mud that gurgles along the road bed.
The thick elastic mud that is kneaded and pounded and squeezed under
the hoofs of the horses;
The invincible inexhaustible mud of the war zone.

This is the song of the mud, the uniform of the poilu.
His coat is of mud, his great dragging coat that is too big for him and
too heavy;
His coat that once was blue and now is grey and stiff with the mud
that cakes to it.
This is the mud that clothes him. His trousers and boots are of mud,
And his skin is of mud;
And there is mud in his beard.
His head is crowned with a helmet of mud.
He wears it well.
He wears it as a king wears the ermine that bores him.
He has set a new style in clothing;
He has introduced the chic of mud.
This is the song of the mud that wriggles its way into battle.
The impertinent, the intrusive, the ubiquitous, the unwelcome,
The slimy inveterate nuisance,
That fills the trenches,
That mixes in with the food of the soldiers,
That spoils the working of motors and crawls into their secret parts,

That spreads itself over the guns,
That sucks the guns down and holds them fast in its slimy voluminous lips,
That has no respect for destruction and muzzles the bursting shells;
And slowly, softly, easily,
Soaks up the fire, the noise; soaks up the energy and the courage;
Soaks up the power of armies;
Soaks up the battle.
Just soaks it up and thus stops it.
This is the hymn of mud - the obscene, the filthy, the putrid,
The vast liquid grave of our armies. It has drowned our men.
Its monstrous distended belly reeks with the undigested dead.
Our men have gone into it, sinking slowly, and struggling and slowly
disappearing.
Our fine men, our brave, strong, young men;
Our glowing red, shouting, brawny men.
Slowly, inch by inch, they have gone down into it,
Into its darkness, its thickness, its silence.
Slowly, irresistibly, it drew them down, sucked them down,
And they were drowned in thick, bitter, heaving mud.
Now it hides them, Oh, so many of them!
Under its smooth glistening surface it is hiding them blandly.
There is not a trace of them.
There is no mark where they went down.
The mute enormous mouth of the mud has closed over them.

This is the song of the mud,
The beautiful glistening golden mud that covers the hills like satin;
The mysterious gleaming silvery mud that is spread like enamel over
the valleys.
Mud, the disguise of the war zone;
Mud, the mantle of battles;
Mud, the smooth fluid grave of our soldiers:
This is the song of the MUD.

"The Church, Zillebeke" - October 1918

Mud
Everywhere -
Nothing but mud.
The very air seems thick with it
The few tufts of grass are all smeared with it-
Mud!
The Church a heap of it;
One look, and weep for it.
That's what they've made of it -

Mud!
Slimy and wet
Churned and upset;
Here bones that once mattered
With crosses lie scattered,
Broken and battered,
Covered in mud,
Here, where the Church's bell
Tolled when our heroes fell
In that mad start of hell -
Mud!
That's all that's left of it - mud!
by William Orpen (Official War Artist)

L/Cpl Alfred Miller volunteered from home in New Zealand and was killed in action on the Somme 16 September 1916.

"**Mud**" by Alfred Miller

It's said that our fight with the Kaiser
Is the wettest affray since the Flood,
At least every day makes us wiser
In the infinite samples of mud.
We've mud on our knees and our faces,
We've mud on our ears and our hair,
We've mud that is dreadfully sticky
(Its depth may be more than a foot).
We've mud that is chalky and tricky,
We've mud that is liquefied soot.

At times we have mud that's like treacle,
At times it is thinner than soup,
At times many men by a squeak'll
Just fail to do 'looping the loop'.
No matter what else may befall us,
No matter how smooth be our path,
When home the authorities call us,
The first thing we'll need is a BATH.

Robert Service came from a Scottish family; started as a bank clerk; to Yukon when 21, travelled widely and wrote comic verse. War correspondent for the Toronto Star in Balkan War of 1912-13, then to Paris. In 1914 falsely arrested as a spy in Dunkirk; though nearly 41, he tried to join the Seaforth Highlanders but failed for medical reasons (varicose veins) so became a war correspondent, stretcher bearer and ambulance driver at the Front, with the American Red Cross Ambulance service, which inspired many of his war poems.

"A Song Of Winter Weather" by Robert Service

It isn't the foe that we fear
It isn't the bullets that whine
It isn't the business career
Of a shell or the use of a mine
It isn't the snipers who seek
To nip our young hopes in the bud
No it isn't the guns
And it isn't the Huns
It's the MUD - MUD - MUD

It isn't the melee we mind.
That often is rather good fun.
It isn't the shrapnel we find
Obtrusive when rained by the ton;
It isn't the bounce of the bombs
That gives us a positive pain:
It's the strafing we get
When the weather is wet -
It's the RAIN - RAIN - RAIN.

It isn't because we lack grit
We shrink from the horrors of war.
We don't mind the battle a bit
In fact that is what we are for
It isn't the rum-jars and things
Make us wish we were back in the fold
It's the fingers that freeze
In the boreal breeze -
It's the COLD - COLD - COLD.

Oh, the rain, the mud, and the cold,
The cold, the mud, and the rain;
With weather at zero it's hard for a hero
From language that's rude to refrain.
With porridge muck to the knees,
With sky that's a-pouring a flood,
Sure the worst of our foes
Are the pains and the woes
Of the RAIN,
the COLD,
and the MUD.

Robert Service.

FAMILY, BEREAVEMENT & MOURNING

Ivor Gurney's dear friend Willy Harvey had gone missibg, presumed dead. In fact he had been taken prisoner while foolishly walking along an empty German trench. News later came through that he was alive, a prisoner of war, but Ivor still wrote a poem mourning him.

"To His Love"

He's gone, and all our plans
  Are useless indeed.
We'll walk no more on Cotswold
  Where sheep feed
  Quietly and take no heed.

His body that was so quick
  Is not as you
Knew it, on Severn river
  Under the blue
  Driving our small boat through.

You would not know him now...
  But still he died
Nobly, so cover him over
  With violets of pride
  Purple from Severn side.

Cover him, cover him soon!
  And with thick-set
Masses of memoried flowers -
  Hide that red wet
  Thing I must somehow forget.

Gurney made several drafts, and toyed with many alternative lines. The genuine grief expressed suggests that the concept came to him when he heard the bad news, and before he knew Harvey was safe as a prisoner of war - though the first manuscript we have is dated January 1917, apparently an error for 1918!

"The Fire Kindled"

God, that I might see
  Framilode once again!
Redmarley, all renewed,
  Clear shining after rain.

And Cranham, Cranham trees,
  And blaze of Autumn hues.

Portway under the moon,
 Silvered with freezing dews.

May Hill that Gloster dwellers
 'Gainst every sunset see;
And the wide Severn river
 Homing again to the sea.
The star of afterglow,
 Venus, on western hills;
Dymock in spring: O Spring
 Of home! O daffodils!

And Malvern's matchless huge
 Bastions of ancient fires -
These will not let me rest,
 So hot my heart desires ....

Here we go sore of shoulder,
 Sore of foot, by quiet streams;
But these are not my rivers
 And these are useless dreams.

I.G. October 1916

"The Signaller's Vision"

One rainy winter dusk
 Mending a parting cable,
Sudden I saw so clear
 Home and the tea-table.

So clear it was, so sweet,
 I did not start, but drew
The breath of deep content
 Some minutes ere I knew

My Mother's face that's soother
 Than autumn half-lights kind,
My softly smiling sisters
 Who keep me still in mind,

Were but a dream, a vision -
 That faded. And I knew
The smell of trench, trench-feeling -
 And turned to work anew.

I.G. 8 November 1916

Gurney's Battalion moved south from Laventie towards Albert and the Somme sector, spending Christmas at Thiépval.

"The Strong Thing"

I have seen Death in the faces of men in fear
 Of Death, and shattered, terribly ruined flesh,
Appalled; but through the horror, coloured and clear
 The love of my county, Gloster, rises afresh.
And on the Day of Days, the Judgement Day,
 The Word of Doom awaiting breathless and still,
I'll marvel how sweet's the air down Framilode way,
 And take my sentence on sheer-down Crickley Hill.

I.G. 22 December 1916

"To an Unknown Lady"

You that were once so sweet, art sweeter now
That an even leaden greyness clouds my days;
A pain it is to think on your sweet ways,
Your careless-tender speaking, tender and low.
When the hills enclosed us, hid in happy valleys,
Greeting a thousand times the things most dear,
We wasted thoughts of love in laughter clear,
And told our passion out in mirthful sallies.
But in me now a burning impulse rages
To praise our love in words like flaming gold,
Molten and live for ever; not fit for cold
And coward like-to-passions Time assuages.
Nor do I fear you are lovely only in dreams,
Being as the sky reflected in clear streams.

I.G. 22 December 1916 - Somme

Ivor's empathy with his fellow men.

"The Estaminet"

The crowd of us were drinking
 One night at Riez Bailleul,
The glasses were a-clinking,
 The estaminet was full.

And loud with song and story
 And blue with tales and smoke, -
We spoke no word of glory,
 Nor mentioned "foreign yoke."

But yarns of girls in Blighty;
  Vain, jolly, ugly, fair,
Standoffish, foolish, flighty -
  And O! that we were there!

Where never thuds a "Minnie,"
  But Minnie smiles at you
A-meeting in the spinney,
  With kisses not a few

And of an inn that Johnson
  Does keep; the "Rising Sun."
His friends call him Jack Johnson,
  He's Gloster's only one.

And talk of poacher's habits
  (But girls ever and again)
Of killing weasels, rabbits,
Stoats, pheasants, never men.

Although we knew tomorrow
  Must take us to the line,
In beer hid thought and sorrow,
  In ruddy and white wine.
When all had finished drinking,
  Though still was clear each head,
We said no word - went slinking
  Straight homeward, into bed (?)

O never lads were merrier,
  Nor straighter nor more fine,
Though we were only "Terrier"
  And only, "Second Line."

O I may get to Blighty,
  Or hell, without a sign
Of all the love that filled me,
  Leave dumb the love that filled me,
The flood of love that filled me
  For these dear comrades of mine.

I.G. January 1917

"Song"

Only the wanderer
  Knows England's graces,
Or can anew see clear
  Familiar faces.

And who loves joy as he
  That dwells in shadows?
Do not forget me quite,
  O Severn meadows.

I.G. Courlaincourt, 18 January 1917

Vera Brittain sees off her new fiancé, Roland Leighton:
23 August 1915 - St Pancras Station

"One long sweet kiss pressed close upon my lips,
  One moment's rest on your swift-beating heart,
And all was over, for the hour had come
  For us to part."

Vera never saw Roland again, 4 months later he was dead.

"Roundel" ('Died of Wounds')

Because you died, I shall not rest again,
  But wander ever through the lone world wide,
Seeking the shadow of a dream grown vain
  Because you died.

I shall spend brief and idle hours beside
  The many lesser loves that still remain,
But find in none my triumph and my pride;

And disillusion's slow corroding stain
  Will creep upon each quest but newly tried,
For every striving now shall nothing gain
  Because you died.

Vera Brittain

To R.A.L. Died of wounds, Louvencourt 23 December 1915:

"Perhaps"

Perhaps some day the sun will shine again,
And I shall see that still the skies are blue,
And feel once more I do not live in vain,
Although bereft of You.
Perhaps the golden meadows at my feet
Will make the sunny hours of Spring seem gay,
And I shall find the white May blossoms sweet,
Though you have passed away.
Perhaps the summer woods will shimmer bright,
And crimson roses once again be fair,
And autumn harvest fields a rich delight,
Although you are not there.
Perhaps some day I shall not shrink in pain
To see the passing of the dying year,
And listen to the Christmas songs again
Although You cannot hear.
But, though kind Time may many joys renew,
There is one greatest joy I shall not know
Again, because my heart for loss of You
Was broken, long ago.

Vera Brittain. February 1916

Vera then lost two of her best friends, and her only brother...

"In Memoriam G.R.Y.T."

Sonnet for Geoffrey Thurlow, k.i.a. 23 April 1917, at Monchey-le-Preux

I spoke with you but seldom, yet there lay
Some nameless glamour in your written word,
And thoughts of you rose often - longings stirred
By dear remembrance of the sad blue-grey
That dwelt within your eyes, the even sway
Of your young god-like gait, the rarely heard
But frank bright laughter, hallowed by a Day
That made of Youth Right's offering to the sword.
So now I ponder, since your day is done,
Ere dawn was past, on all you meant to me,
And all the more you might have come to be,
And wonder if some state, beyond the sun
And shadows here, may yet completion see
Of intimacy sweet though scarce begun.

"Sic Transit"

for Victor Richardson, blinded Vimy Ridge, April 1917, died 9 June 1917

I am so tired.
The dying sun incarnadines the West,
And every window with its gold is fired,
And all I loved the best
Is gone, and every good that I desired
Passes away, an idle hopeless quest;
Even the Highest whereto I aspired
Has vanished with the rest.
I am so tired.

Vera Brittain

Five poems dedicated to Vera's brother Edward Brittain:

Written 11 June 1918, commemorating the MC he won two years earlier, 1 July 1916, the first day of the "Somme." When wounded, Edward was sent to the same hospital in London where Vera was a VAD.

"To My Brother"

Your battle-wounds are scars upon my heart,
Received when in that grand and tragic 'show'
You played your part
Two years ago,
And silver in the summer morning sun
I see the symbol of your courage glow-
That Cross you won
Two years ago.

Though now again you watch the shrapnel fly,
And hear the guns that daily louder grow,
As in July
Two years ago.
May you endure to lead the Last Advance
And with your men pursue the flying foe
As once in France
Two years ago.

Alas, Edward did not endure, but was killed only four days after Vera wrote this, 15 June 1918.

"Then And Now"

Once the black pine-trees on the mountain side,
 The river dancing down the valley blue,
And strange brown grasses swaying with the tide,
 All spake to me of you.
But now the sullen streamlet creeping slow,
 The moaning tree-tops dark above my head,
The weeds where once the grasses used to grow
 Tell me that you are dead.

"The Only Son"

The storm beats loud, and you are far away,
 The night is wild,
On distant fields of battle breaks the day,
 My little child?

I sought to shield you from the least of ills
 In bygone years,
I scooted with dreams of manhood's far-off hills
 Your baby fears.

But could not save you from the shock of strife;
 With radiant eyes
You seized the sword and in the path of Life
 You sought your prize.

The tempests rage, but you are fast asleep;
 Though winds be wild
They cannot break your endless slumbers deep,
 My little child.

Vera Brittain

"Epitaph for Edward"

Not where the golden sunshine softly smiles
Upon the fields of your lost Happy Isles
You wait for me. Your joyous songs are stilled.
For to the sunset land of Avalon
You and your music and your dreams are gone,
Not here, dear child, not here to be fulfilled.

Vera Brittain

"**Lamplight**" by May Wedderburn Cannan

For her fiancé, Bevil Quiller-Couch, died of Spanish Flu, 1919

We planned to shake the world together, you and I
Being young, and very wise:
Now in the light of the green shaded lamp
Almost I see your eyes
Light with the old gay laughter; you and I
Dreamed greatly of an Empire in those days,
Setting our feet upon laborious ways,
And all you asked of fame
Was crossed swords in the Army List,
My Dear, against your name.

We planned a great Empire together, you and I
Bound only by the sea;
Now in the quiet of a chill Winter's night
Your voice comes hushed to me
Full of forgotten memories; you and I
Dreamed great dreams of our future in those days,
Setting our feet on undiscovered ways,
And all I asked of fame
A scarlet cross on my breast, my Dear,
For the swords by your name.

We shall never shake the world together, you and I,
For you gave your life away;
And I think my heart was broken by the war,
Since on a summer day
You took the road we never spoke of: you and I
Dreamed greatly of an Empire in those days;
You set your feet upon the Western ways
And have no need of fame -
There's a scarlet cross on my breast, my Dear,
And a torn cross with your name.

M.W.C.

"The Falling Leaves" by Margaret Postgate Cole

Today, as I rode by,
I saw the brown leaves dropping from their tree
In a still afternoon,
When no wind whirled them whistling to the sky,
But thickly, silently,
They fell, like snowflakes wiping out the noon;
And wandered slowly thence
For thinking of a gallant multitude
Which now all withering lay,
Slain by no wind of age or pestilence,
But in their beauty strewed
Like snowflakes falling on the Flemish clay.
November 1915

"The Veteran"

We came upon him sitting in the sun -
Blinded by war, and left. And past the fence
Wandered young soldiers from the Hand & Flower,
Asking advice of his experience.
And he said this and that, and told them tales;
And all the nightmares of each empty head
Blew into air. Then, hearing us beside -
"Poor kids, how do they know what it's like?" he said.
And we stood there, and watched him as he sat
Turning his sockets where they went away;
Until it came to one of us to ask
"And you're - how old?"
"Nineteen the third of May."
by Margaret Postgate Cole

"After the War"

After the war perhaps I'll sit again
Out on the terrace where I sat with you,
And see the changeless sky and hills beat blue
And live an afternoon of summer through.

I shall remember then, and sad at heart
For the lost day of happiness we knew,
Wish only that some other man were you
And spoke my name as once you used to do.
by May Wedderburn Cannan

Marian Allen was set to marry Arthur Greg, who was studying law at Oxford with her brother Dundas. In 1914 they both left studying to fight, Arthur at Hill 60, Belgium, until badly wounded in May 1915. When recovered he joined Dundas in the Royal Flying Corps, but was shot down and killed on a bombing raid over St.Quentin, 23 April 1917.

Ten days after she heard the news of Arthur's death, on 10 May, 1917, Marian wrote these two sonnets, now combined:

"The Wind on the Downs"

I like to think of you as brown and tall,
As strong and living as you used to be,
In khaki tunic, Sam Brown belt and all,
And standing there and laughing down at me.
Because they tell me, dear, that you are dead,
Because I can no longer see your face,
You have not died, it is not true, instead
You seek adventure some other place.
That you are round about me, I believe;
I hear you laughing as you used to do,
Yet loving all the things I think of you;
And knowing you are happy, should I grieve?
You follow and are watchful where I go;
How should you leave me, having loved me so?

We walked along the towpath, you and I,
Beside the sluggish-moving, still canal;
It seemed impossible that you should die;
I think of you the same and always shall.
We thought of many things and spoke of few,
And life lay all uncertainly before,
And now I walk alone and think of you,
And wonder what new kingdoms you explore.
Over the railway line, across the grass,
While up above the golden wings are spread,
Flying, ever flying overhead,
Here still I see your khaki figure pass,
And when I leave the meadow, almost wait,
That you should open first the wooden gate.

Marian Allen

Marian composed this for her beloved Arthur Greg, 6 months after he was killed:

"Out in a Gale of Fallen Leaves" by Marian Allen

Out in a gale of fallen leaves,
Where the wind blows clear through the rain-soaked trees,
Where the sky is torn betwixt cloud and blue
And the rain but ceases to fall anew:
And dead leaves, in bud on your April flight,
Will whisper your name to the wind to-night
And the year is dying in which you died
And I shall be lonely this Christmas-tide.
Marian Allen, Hyde Park Oct 1917

American Mary Borden used her wealth to build an evacuation hospital near the front line in France, which she ran. One day, in 1916, an exhausted English officer, Captain Louis Spears, knocked on her door. They fell in love. She divorced her first husband, so they could get married, in 1918. As well as 'The Song of the Mud' she wrote 10 private love sonnets for Spears, two printed here:

"Sonnet I"

What more can the desolate murmuring sea
Say to my heart, since you have kissed my lips?
What terror does it hold, what mystery
That I ignore?
Those far white phantom ships
Riding the dim horizon to the south
Travel no father than my fearful soul
Each night that I lie clinging to your mouth -
Then in your arms I cross from pole to pole
The sobbing waste, I visit the pale moon
And learn the hopeless passion of the tide.
Dive down to guilty caverns; in a swoon
Drift up again and of a sudden ride
Stupendous storms until at last I lie
Dying upon your heart and glad to die -
Mary Borden xxx

"Sonnet VIII"

Because we know that there will never be
Any more time when this our time is done,
Because we know there is for you and me
No other place under another sun
And that our day is bounded by a night
Impenetrably dark, boundlessly deep
Let this our fearful day be full of light
Let this our day be sweet.
Let us be glad for this our little time
More glad than ever lovers were before
And let us dare to fashion the sublime
Within the ghostly chasm of the war
Standing together in the roaring gloom
At peace before our sure advancing doom.

Mary Borden

She needn't have worried, she and Spears were married for 50 years!
She also wrote "The Forbidden Zone" and several novels. In Beirut, in WW2, Spears became an emissary of his friend Winston Churchill.

"The Gift of India" by Sarojini Naidu - August 1915

Nearly 150,000 (1 in 10 of the Indian troops in the British army in WWI) were casualties. Naidu, friend of Ghandi, was the first woman President of the Indian National Congress, in 1925.

Is there aught you need that my hands withhold,
Rich gifts of raiment or grain or gold?
Lo! I have flung to the East and West
Priceless treasures torn from my breast,
And yielded the sons of my stricken womb
To the drum-beats of duty, the sabres of doom.

Gathered like pearls in their alien graves
Silent they sleep by the Persian waves,
Scattered like shells on Egyptian sands,
They lie with pale brows and brave, broken hands,
They are strewn like blossoms mown down by chance
On the blood-brown meadows of Flanders and France.
Can ye measure the grief of the tears I weep
Or compass the woe of the watch I keep?
Or the pride that thrills thro' my heart's despair,
And the hope that comforts the anguish of prayer?
And the far sad glorious vision I see

Of the torn red banners of Victory?

When the terror and tumult of hate shall cease
And life be refashioned on anvils of peace,
And your love shall offer memorial thanks
To the comrades who fought in your dauntless ranks,
And you honour the deeds of the deathless ones
Remember the blood of thy martyred sons!
Sarojini Naidu

Love poem for fiancé Bevil Quiller-Couch MC, who fought the whole war, 1914-18, only to die of Spanish Flu in 1919.

"English Leave" by May Cannan

Kneel then in the warm lamplight, O my Love,
Your dear dark head against my quiet breast,
And take me in your arms again and so
Hush my tired heart to rest;
And say that of all the glories you have won
My love's most dear and best.
Only to-night I want you all my own,
(Tomorrow I will laugh and bid you go,)
That if these fourteen days of heaven on earth
Are all the love-time we shall ever know
I may remember I am yours: My Dear,
Hold me still closer, still ... and tell me so.

"Haumont Wood, 1918" by Louise Bogan

O you so long dead,
You masked and obscure,
I can tell you, all things endure:
The wine and the bread;

The marble quarried for the arch;
The iron become steel;
The spoke broken from the wheel;
The sweat of the long march;

The hay-stacks cut through like loaves
And the hundred flowers from the seed;
All things indeed
Though struck by the hooves

Of disaster, of time due,
Of fell loss and gain,
All things remain,
I can tell you, this is true.

Though burned down to stone
Though lost from the eye,
I can tell you, and not lie,--
Save of peace alone.

"Soldier-Poet" by Hervey Allen

To Francis Hogan, poet-friend, k.i.a. in the Argonne, Oct. 1918

I think at first like us he did not see
The goal to which the screaming eagles flew;
For romance lured him, France, and chivalry;
But oh! Before the end he knew, he knew!
And gave his first full love to Liberty,
And met her face to face one lurid night
While the guns boomed their shuddering minstrelsy
And all the Argonne glowed with demon light.
And Liberty herself came through the wood,
And with her dear, boy lover kept the tryst;
Clasped in her grand, Greek arms he understood
Whose were the fatal lips that he had kissed -
Lips that the soul of Youth has loved from old -
Hot lips of Liberty that kiss men cold.

Gassed, burned and wounded in August, Allen was evacuated and escaped the battle of Argonne, and so survived the war.

"A Song and a Smile" by Robert Beckh

Meet life with a smile
Tho' the long road be rough,
Full many a mile,
If you're of the right stuff,
You'll find you can wile
With a song and a smile.
Come danger, come Death,
Set teeth and brace back.

Still woo Mother Earth
Tho' her brows be bent black,
With a smile full of mirth,
And she'll soon pay you back
In the coin that you're worth.
Be there sorrow or Death
Let your smile linger still,
Tho' there's sadness beneath
Keep it there at your will;
Have a smile while you've breath,
For your friends it will fill
With contempt of King Death.

The day after composing this poem, 15 August 1916, Beckh led two patrols in No Man's Land, but was killed by machine-gun fire.

"No-Man's Land" by J L Brown

A father who has been searching No Man's Land every night for a week for the body of his son.

After the long weeks, my son, we meet at last.
The times have gone above us both so fast - so fast
That but an eyelid's fall would seem to span
The years that changed you from a boy to man ...
You with the blossom-face, and eyes of wonder,
Blue as the strange new skies you wandered under,
All was so fresh to you - the world a toy -
Vivid, bewildering, delightful boy ...
You with new knowledge and the heart of youth
For ever seeking the eternal Truth ...
Child - boy - man - all that my heart held dear -
All that was you - except the soul - lies here.

So strangely still! And I to see your face
Must creep in darkness to this fateful place,
The dreadful midst, where but to raise a head
Will add another to the unburied dead,

Where noiselessly a dozen yards away
Nerve-shattered men await the dawning day,
And search, with fingers twitching on their triggers
For fancied forms and fear-created figures.

Ah, you are wise and quiet! Saner far
Than these poor shaken desperate creatures are,
Or I, who crouch beneath the scudding sky

Ready to kill, or, failing that, to die,
Flattening myself like any hunted hare
Beneath the moonlight and the star-shell's flare.
God! Has the world gone mad that men should creep
To slay an unknown brother in his sleep!
This silent congregation is more wise
Than all live things which crawl beneath the skies.
Gropingly in the dark my fingers trace
Each feature of the well-remembered face ...
The firm young mouth, straight nose, and boyish brow,
The eyes whose wonderment is over now
(The night lies heavy on their dawning blue);
For the last time I run my fingers through
The fair young locks, sun-kissed and touched to gold ...
For the last time my fingers find and hold
Those strong young fingers, now so cold - so cold!
A week, my son, I sought the place you fell;
Now I have found you. Greeting and farewell!

O God, whose son was mangled on a tree,
By my poor mangled son I pray to Thee:
Let peace and pity ring this earth about,
Or send thy thunderbolts and blot us out!

John L C Brown

Weaving gained a double first at Oxford in Classics and Maths and was mentored in his poetry by Robert Bridges. A schoolmaster, he volunteered as a Lieutenant in 1915, but was evacuated from France with heart failure that September, and discharged.

"Between the Trenches" by Willoughby Weaving

A soldier regards his newly-killed friend.

How strangely did you break upon
That sudden land beyond life's veil?
A moment did your spirit fail,
As mine when first I knew you gone
The last dark journey, saw your clay
So vacant, loveless, borne away,
And the features, that I loved to scan,
The same but of another man
Unknown - a bright dream all undone.

What stranger did the bearers lift
In their soiled stretcher lightly laid
Where I had seen you fall adrift

From life - had time to be afraid?
- That, all of you that had breathed and moved
That, none of you that lived and loved,
A hush that so I seemed to hate
For claiming still its lost inmate,
A false pretence, a solid shade.
Shadow more solid, but less real
Than love and laughter whence it fell
Across my path with mute appeal
And served your spirit's purpose well -
So well that even I could see
It indistinguishably thee,
Till you had left it like a sheath
With laughter in the hands of death,
And left me gay, not miserable.
Ah, love had never more to lose:
If certain love had less to tell
Then might I in despair's excuse
Bid you a hopeless, vain farewell,
And by the stranger's grave have wept
A solemn while, and sadly kept
In mind his features filled not through
With breathing life, love living, you
Who smiled upon his burial.

W Weaving

Marc De Larreguy De Civrieux, *killed at Froideterre, Verdun, 18 November 1916*

"Le Drapeau De La Révolte" - March 1916

I call in your name, Brothers in obscurity,
Who fear to shout aloud your grievous sufferings,
But die without a word or hope of better things,
For the dishonoured Leaders of humanity!
I call in your name, Parents weeping bitterly
To mourn a son, for whom death liberation brings:
You can believe no more, smarting from sorrow's stings,
In your false Torturers, who dupe you constantly!
I call in your name, comrades silent in the tomb
As endlessly you swell the senseless hecatomb,
But on the Day of Truth will rise triumphantly!

It is in all your names that I address my call
For people everywhere to raise, as Nations fall,
The Banner of Revolt and of Fraternity.

Two victims of Turkey's 1915 Armenian Massacres, when over a million Armenians were murdered:

"The Flickering Lamp" by Daniel Varouzan

This is a night for feast and triumph,
Pour oil into the lamp, O Bride,
My boy returns a victor from war -
Trim well, trim well the wick, O Bride.

A wagon stops before the door, beside the well,
Light up, light up the lamp, O Bride,
My boy returns, bay leaves on his brow -
Bring up, bring up the lamp, O Bride.

Lo - with grief and blood the wagon's laden -
Hold up, hold up the lamp, O Bride.
Here lies my valiant son, shot through the heart -
O ... snuff out, snuff out the lamp, O Bride.

Siamanto, another of the 761 Armenian intellectuals massacred in Constantinople in 1915:

"A Handful Of Ash"

Alas, you were a great and beautiful mansion,
And from the white summit of your roof,
Filled with star-flooded night hopes,
I listened to the Euphrates, racing below.

I learned with tears, with tears I learned of the ruins,
Of your broad walls battered down, stone by stone,
On to your fragile border of flowers in the garden ...
On a terror-filled day, a day of slaughter, of blood.

And charred is the blue room
Inside whose walls, on whose rugs
My childhood delighted
And where my life grew where my soul grew

That gold-framed mirror is shattered too
In whose silver depth my dreams
My hopes my loves and my burning will
Stood reflected for years and my musings

And in the garden the spring song is dead,
The mulberry and the willow there, they have been blasted, too,
And the brook that flowed between the trees -
Has it gone dry? Tell me, where is it? Has it gone dry?

O I often dream of the cage
From which my grey partridge, mornings
And at sunrise, fronting the rose trees -
Would rise, as I did, and start its own distinct cooing.

O my homeland, promise that after my death
A handful of your holy ashes
Will come to rest, like an exiled turtledove,
To chant its song of sorrow and tears.

But who will bring me, tell me, who is to bring
A handful of your precious ashes,
On the day of my death, to put into my dark coffin
And mingle with my ashes, ashes of a singer of the homeland?

A handful of ash with my remains, my native home -
Who is to bring a handful of ash from your ashes,
From your sorrow, your memories, your past;
A handful of ash to scatter on my heart?
Siamento [pseudonym of Atom Earčanian]

"The Soldier's Son"

The little boy whose innocent yellow head
Has bobbed among the buttercups all day,
The earth being silent now and the light shed,
Kneels down to pray.
And, full of faith, he knows that God will keep
Safe one who lies
Feeding the rats that with the shadows creep
And husbanding the flies.
Theodore H. van Beek - 1917

Lt. Dennis Day was shot by a sniper at Vermelles on 25 Sept 1915. His brother Jeffery, a keen pilot, at Dunkirk, won the DSO in January 1918 for attacking 6 German planes single-handed, and then wrote this poem:

"To My Brother"

At first when unaccustomed to death's sting
I thought that should you die each sweetest thing,
each thing of any merit on this earth
would perish also, beauty love and mirth:
and that the world despoiled and God-forsaken
its glories gone its greater treasures taken
would sink into a slough of apathy

and there remain into eternity,
a mournful-minded, soul-destroying place
wherein there would be seen no smiling face,
where all desire to love and live would cease,
and death would be the only way to peace.
And when one day the aching blow did fall
for many days I did not live at all,
but, dazed and halting, made my endless way
painfully though a tangled growth of grey
and clinging thorns, dismal, towards belief,
and uncontrollable, heart-racking grief.
It could not be! – that one so fair and strong,
so honest-minded, and so void of wrong,
that one who made such splendid use of life,
whose smile could soothe the bitterness of strife
and make a cold, hard nature warm and soft
(who used to smile so frankly and so oft)
should die, and leave our spirits numb and breaking,
grief-stifled, and yet empty, sick, and breaking.
I prayed that God might give me power to sever
your sad remembrance from my mind forever.
"Never again shall I have heart to do
the things in which we took delight, we two.
I cannot bear the cross. Oh, to forget
the haunting vision of the past!": and yet
surely it were a far more noble thing
to keep your memories all fresh as spring,
to do again the things that we held dear
and thus to feel your spirit ever near.
This will I do when peace shall come again—
peace and return, to ease my heart of pain.
Crouched in the brittle reed-beds, wrapped in grey
I'll watch the dawning of the winter's day,
the peaceful, clinging darkness of the night
that mingles with the mystic morning light,
and graceful rushes, melting in the haze,
while all around in winding water ways
the wild fowl gabble cheerfully and low
or wheel with pulsing whistle to and fro,
filling the silent dawn with sweetest song,
swelling and dying as they sweep along,
till shadows of vague trees deceive the eyes,
and stealthily the sun begins to rise,
striving to smear with pink the frosted sky
and pierce the silver mist's opacity;

until the hazy silhouettes grow clear
and faintest hints of colouring appear,
and the slow, throbbing, red, distorted sun
reaches the sky, and all the large mists run,
leaving the little ones to wreathe and shiver,
pathetic, clinging to the friendly river;
until the watchful heron, grim and gaunt,
shows ghostlike, standing at his favourite haunt,
and jerkily the moorhens venture out,
spreading swift, circled ripples round about;
and softly to the ear, and leisurely,
querulous, comes the plaintive plover's cry.
And then, maybe, some whispering near by,
some still, small, sound as of a happy sigh
shall steal upon my senses, soft as air,
and, brother! I shall know that thou ar[t] there.
Then, with my gun forgotten in my hand,
I'll wander through the snow-encrusted land,
following the tracks of hare and stoat, and traces
of bird and beast, as delicate as laces,
doing again the things that we held dear,
keeping thy gracious spirit ever near,
comforted by the blissful certainty
and sweetness of thy splendid company.

And in the lazy summer nights I'll glide
silently down the sleepy river's tide,
listening to the music of the stream,
the plop of ponderously playful bream,
the water whispering around the boat,
and from afar the white owl's liquid note
that lingers through the stillness, soft and slow;
watching the little yacht's red homely glow,
her vague reflection, and her clean cut spars
ink-black against the stillness of the stars,
stealthily slipping into nothingness,
while on the river's moon-splashed surfaces
tall shadows sweep.
Then, when I go to rest,
it may be that my slumbers will be blest
by the faint sound of thy untroubled breath,
proving thy presence near, in spite of death.

by Jeffery Day

27 February 1918, just 21, after 5 more victories in his Sopwith Camel, Jeffery Day was shot down over the North Sea by 6 German aircraft - so he never got to commune with his brother's spirit in the Fens.

Billy Grenfell joined up when War broke, also fought in Belgium, less than a mile from his brother; he was k.i.a. two months after Julian - 30 July 1915 - his name is listed on the Menin Gate.

"To John" by William Grenfell

'John' was J Manners, his friend in the BEF, killed 1 September 1914

O heart-and-soul and careless played
  Our little band of brothers,
And never recked the time would come
  To change our games for others.
It's joy for those who played with you
  To picture now what grace
Was in your mind and single heart
  And in your radiant face.
Your light-foot strength by flood and field
  For England keener glowed;
To whatever things are fair
  We know, through you, the road;
Nor is our grief the less thereby;
  O swift and strong and dear, good-bye.

"As I Came Up From Wiper" by J C Hobson

As I came up from Wipers
  Before the break of day,
When silver rain was falling
  And the light was silver grey,
I heard a cock start crowing,
  And I heard a bugle call,
And I heard a throstle singing,
  On a ruined ivied wall.

The mists were on the meadows,
  The dew was on the flowers,
The early sun had touched with gold
  The graceful ruined towers.
But my heart was sad and heavy,
  My mind was full of care,
For thinking of a laddie
  Who was lying buried there.

Oh! laddie, can ye hear me?
  Do you mind that winter's day
When you and I together
  Marched up the self-same way?
Our hearts were strong and cheery,
  Our faces hard and set
Ay, laddie, you remember!
  And I shall not forget!
        k.i.a. at St.Julien, Ypres, 31 July 1917

Private Thomas Clayton, died of wounds 31 August 1918

"The Casualty List" by T Clayton

'Killed - Wounded - Missing. Officers and men,
  So many hundreds.' Numbers leave us cold.
  But when next day the tale again is told
In serried lines of printed names - Ah then!
The tragic meaning of it all grows plain.
We know them not; yet picture in each one
  Some woman's husband, some fond mother's son,
Some maiden's lover, some child's father - slain!

The cost of war looms large before our eyes;
Our hearts beat quicker, tears unbidden rise.
Then thoughts fly upward, shape themselves in prayer
'God of our fathers, for the stricken care!
The wounded do Thou heal, the lost restore;
Bind broken hearts, bid mourners weep no more;
Loved ones in peril guard by day and night;
And speed, O Lord, the triumph of the Right!'

Lt. J H Wickersham, killed in action, St.Mihiel, September 12, 1918.

"The Raindrops On Your Old Tin Hat" by Lt. J H Wickersham

The mist hangs low and quiet on a ragged line of hills,
  There's a whispering of wind across the flat,
You'd be feeling kind of lonesome if it wasn't for one thing
The patter of the raindrops on your old tin hat.

An' you just can't help a-figuring - sitting there alone -
  About this war and hero stuff and that,
And you wonder if they haven't sort of got things twisted up,
  While the rain keeps its patter on your old tin hat.

When you step off with the outfit to do your little bit,
  You're simply doing what you're s'posed to do -
And you don't take time to figure what you gain or lose -
  It's the spirit of the game that brings you through.

But back at home she's waiting, writing cheerful little notes,
  And every night she offers up a prayer
And just keeps on a-hoping that her soldier boy is safe -
  The Mother of the boy who's over there.

And fellows, she's the hero of this great big ugly war,
  And her prayer is on the wind across the flat,
And don't you reckon maybe it's her tears, and not the rain,
  That's keeping up the patter on your old tin hat?

"To My Daughter Betty, the Gift of God" - (aged 3)

by Lt. Thomas Kettle, Irish MP, barrister, orator, Home Ruler... (Brother-in-law shot, April 1916, at the Easter Rising). This poem composed on 4 Sept 1916; Kettle was killed in the first minute of the attack on Guillemont, Somme, 8 Sept 1916.

In wiser days, my darling rosebud, blown
To beauty proud as was your mother's prime,
In that desired, delayed, incredible time,
You'll ask why I abandoned you, my own,
And the dear heart that was your baby throne,
To dice with death. And oh! They'll give you rhyme
And reason: some will call the thing sublime,
And some decry it in a knowing tone.

So here, while the mad guns curse overhead,
And tired men sigh with mud for couch and floor,
Know that we fools, now with the foolish dead,
Died not for flag, nor King, nor Emperor,
But for a dream, born in a herdsman's shed,
And for the Secret Scripture of the poor.

Last 2 lines refer to Jesus in the stable and show Kettle's deep Christian faith. He, his sister and brother-in-law were all friends of James Joyce.

"**April 1918**" by H C Bradby

Housemaster of School House, at Rugby School, taught Rupert Brooke. Eldest son killed at Arras, April 1917, where Ivor Gurney and Siegfried Sassoon were both wounded and Edward Thomas killed, in the same battle.

You, whose forebodings have been all fulfilled,
You who have heard the bell, seen the boy stand
Holding the flimsy message in his hand
While through your heart the fiery question thrilled
'Wounded or killed, which, which?' - and it was 'Killed' -
And in a kind of trance have read it, numb
But conscious that the dreaded hour was come,
No dream this dream wherewith your blood was chilled -
Oh brothers in calamity, unknown
Companions in the order of black loss,
Lift up your hearts, for you are not alone,
And let our sombre hosts together bring
Their sorrows to the shadow of the Cross
And learn the fellowship of suffering.

Two teachers mourn their former pupils:

"To My Pupils, Gone Before Their Day"

by Guy Kendall, teacher at Charterhouse - Oct 1915, later headmaster of University College School, London.

You seemed so young, to know
So little, those few months or years ago,
Who may by now have disentwined
The inmost secrets of the Eternal Mind.
Yours seemed an easy part,
To construe, learn some trivial lines by heart:

Yet to your hands hath God assigned
The burden of the sorrows of mankind.
You passed the brief school year
In expectation of some long career,
Then yielded up all years to find
That long career that none can leave behind.
If you had lived, some day
You would have passed my room, and chanced to say,
'I wonder if it's worth the grind
Of all those blunders he has underlined.'

Perhaps! If at the end
You in your turn shall teach me how to mend
The many errors whose effect
Eternity awaits to correct.

"Three Hills" by Rev. Everard Owen,
(Teacher at Harrow 'on the hill', Dec 1915)

There is a hill in England,
 Green fields and a school I know,
Where the balls fly fast in summer,
 And the whispering elm-trees grow,
 A little hill, a dear hill,
 And the playing fields below.

There is a hill in Flanders,
 Heaped with a thousand slain,
Where the shells fly night and noontide
 And the ghosts that died in vain,
  A little hill, a hard hill
 To the souls that died in pain.

There is a hill in Jewry,
 Three crosses pierce the sky,
On the midmost He is dying
 To save all those who die,
  A little hill, a kind hill
 To souls in jeopardy.

An Old Harrovian celebrates dying for the honour of his school. Cpt. Rose-Troup was studying law when war broke out and was soon captured at the Battle of Ypres, 1915. These poems written as a German prisoner-of-war in Weilburg an der Lahn, May 1916, and published in 1917.

"Harrow's Honour" by J M Rose-Troup
Let us now praise famous men

A weary time a dreary time, a time of hopes and fears
The weeks that pass the months that pass and lengthen
 into years.
My heart goes back to Harrow, to Harrow far away,
And Harrow sends a message to cheer me on my way.
"For good come, bad come, they came the same before,
So heigh ho, follow the game, and show the way to more."

Mourn not for those whose names are writ in gold,
They fought for England, gladly gave their all.
Kept Harrow's honour spotless as of old,
Nor feared to answer to the last great call.

They showed the way to more, their names will ring
Through all succeeding years of Harrow's fame,
Whatever changes after years may bring
Their sons will follow up and play the game.

O Mother Herga, all our thanks we give
For all your care of us, your watchful eye:
You made us men, you taught us how to live,
And in your wisdom taught us how to die.

The strongest bond of all, the bond of friends
Made in our youth, a bond that naught can break,
Binds us to you until our journey ends,
We live, we fight, we die for Harrow's sake.

William Dyment joined the Royal Engineers in May 1917 and a year later died near Amiens. His son Clifford, born January 1914 was only four when his father died. He found his father's letter when he was 21, in 1935, and wrote this poem:

"The Son" by Clifford Dyment

I found the letter in a cardboard box,
Unfamous history. I read the words.
The ink was pale and brown, the paper dry
After so many years of being kept.
The letter was a soldier's, from the Front -
Conveyed his love, and disappointed hope
Of getting leave. 'It's cancelled now', he wrote.
'My luck is at the bottom of the sea.'

Outside the sun was hot; the world looked bright;
I heard a radio, and someone laughed.
I did not sing, or laugh, or love the sun.
Within the quiet room I thought of him,
My father killed, and all the other men
Whose luck was at the bottom of the sea.

Francis Ledwidge, Irish, the self-styled 'Poet of the Blackbird', left school at 14.

"To One Dead" - 1915

For a girl Ledwidge had once loved, who died in childbirth.

A blackbird singing
On a moss-upholstered stone,
Bluebells swinging,
   Shadows wildly blown,
A song in a wood,
A ship on the sea,
    The song was for you,
    and the ship was for me.

Nor shall he know when loud March blows
Thro' slanting snows her fanfare shrill,
Blowing to flame the golden cup
Of many an upset daffodil.

But when the Dark Cow leaves the moor,
And pastures poor with greedy weeds,
Perhaps he'll hear her low at morn,
Lifting her horn in pleasant meads.

Ledwidge was sent to the Somme, late December 1916. He was bitterly cold, at La Neuville, and 'always homesick'. In April 1917, he moved to the Monchy-le-Preux trenches near Arras, for the Battle (along with Gurney, Sassoon, Thomas et al.)

"At a Poet's Grave"

When I leave down this pipe my friend
And sleep with flowers I loved, apart,
My songs shall rise in wilding things
Whose roots are in my heart.

And here where that sweet poet sleeps
I hear the songs he left unsung,
When winds are fluttering the flowers
And summer-bells are rung.

"The Lost Ones"

Somewhere is music from the linnets' bills,
And thro' the sunny flowers the bee-wings drone,
And white bells of convolvulus on hills
Of quiet May make silent ringing, blown
Hither and thither by the wind of showers,
And somewhere all the wandering birds have flown;
And the brown breath of Autumn chills the flowers.

But where are all the loves of long ago?
O little twilight ship blown up the tide,
Where are the faces laughing in the glow
Of morning years, the lost ones scattered wide?
Give me your hand, O brother, let us go
Crying about the dark for those who died.

Francis Ledwidge

"Home" by Francis Ledwidge

Written a fortnight before he was killed, 31st July 1917

A burst of sudden wings at dawn,
Faint voices in a dreamy noon,
Evenings of mist and murmurings,
And nights with rainbows of the moon.

And through these things a wood-way dim,
And waters dim, and slow sheep seen
On uphill paths that wind away
Through summer sounds and harvest green.

This is a song a robin sang
This morning on a broken tree,
It was about the little fields
That call across the world to me.

Ledwidge was k.i.a. at Pilckem, with fellow poets J Hobson & E Evans - known as "Hedd Wyn" - 31 July 1917, 1st day, 3rd Battle of Ypres, at Passchendaele, three of the 31,000 killed that day; they are buried together in Artillery Wood cemetery.

Ledwidge's last poem was composed 22 July 1917:

"To One Who Comes Now And Then"

When you come in, it seems a brighter fire
Crackles upon the hearth invitingly,
The household routine which was wont to tire
Grows full of novelty.

You sit upon our home-upholstered chair
And talk of matters wonderful and strange,
Of books, and travel, customs old which dare
The gods of Time and Change.

Till we with inner word our care refute
Laughing that this our bosoms yet assails,
While there are maidens dancing to a flute
In Andalusian vales.

And sometimes from my shelf of poems you take
And secret meanings to our hearts disclose,
As when the winds of June the mid bush shake
We see the hidden rose.

And when the shadows muster, and each tree
A moment flutters, full of shutting wings,
You take the fiddle and mysteriously
Wake wonders on the strings.

And in my garden, grey with misty flowers,
Low echoes fainter than a beetle's horn
Fill all the corners with it, like sweet showers
Of bells, in the owl's morn.

Come often, friend, with welcome and surprise
We'll greet you from the sea or from the town;
Come when you like and from whatever skies
Above you smile or frown.

Francis Ledwidge

Robert Vernède was killed leading an advance at Havrincourt, 9 April 1917. The previous day he wrote his last letter, Easter Sunday: '...perhaps the war will end this year and I shall see my Pretty One again.' His dying words were: "Send my love to my wife," his beloved Caroline, to whom he had been married for fifteen years.

"To C.H.V." (Caroline Howard Vernède)

What shall I bring to you, wife of mine,
When I come back from the war?
A ribbon your dear brown hair to twine?
A shawl from a Berlin store?
Say, shall I choose you some Prussian hack
When the Uhlans we overwhelm?
Shall I bring you a Potsdam goblet back
And the crest from a Prince's helm?

Little you'd care what I laid at your feet,
Ribbon or crest or shawl —
What if I bring you nothing, sweet,
Nor maybe come home at all?
Ah, but you'll know, Brave Heart, you'll know
Two things I'll have kept to send:
Mine honour for which you bade me go
And my love - my love to the end.

Robert Ernest Vernède

"In Montauban" by John L C Brown

Quietly now, when the rush and roar of battle is over,
In a wreck of the ruined shell-swept street he lies;
The pangs of death have left no mark but the jaw dropped open,
And patient half-shut eyes.

Sixty winters have left their joys and sorrows upon him,
The hair is silvered which once was brown and thick,
And, near the hand which never shall grasp them living,
Are placed a spade and pick.

Some old gardener, I fancy, who, back in his cottage in England,
Read to his wife on Sunday afternoon,
While the sun came through the blinds, and flowers were fragrant,
And bees were loud in June.

Some old gardener, who, reading that hands were wanted,
Strong and steady and cunning with pick and spade,
Dropped his paper, and went, his tools on his shoulder.
Forth to follow his trade.

So for a time he laboured and hoed and mended,
Stealing forth in the dusk when others sleep,
He and yeomen beside him, who work unknown, unnoticed,
Making the trenches deep.

Then last night through the stars and silences, sudden
A whistle and shattering crash like a thunder-roll,
And through the flying bricks, and the smoke, and the dust, uprising
His startled kindly soul.

So, old friend, in the dawn you pass to a greater sunrise.
Beyond the spite of men who mangle and slay;
And God, Who loves all gardeners, will greet you and bid you enter
His sunnier ampler Day.

Widely and deep I dig, disposing the tools beside him,
Crossing the toil-worn hands and propping the head,
And earth, whose fruits he honoured and worked for living,
Rest on him lightly, dead.

John L C Brown

"Missing: Unofficially Reported Killed" by John L C Brown

Was it noonday that you left us,
 When the ranks were wrapped in smoke?
Or did you pass unnoticed on the midnight,
 Ere the chillier morning broke?

Did the lust and heat of battle find you ready,
 Shoulders braced and hearts aflame?
Or did death steal by and take you unexpected,
 When the final summons came?

Not amidst the companies and clamour
 Or this horror men call War,
Where man, the godlike, tramples down his fellows
 To the dust they were before;

But on some still November morning
 When frost was in the air,
Noiselessly your strong soul took its passing,
 And I, your friend, not there - not there!

Silently the dead leaves swing and settle
 In their appointed place;
The season of the singing birds is over,
 The winter sets apace.

Somewhere in the ruin of the autumn,
 When the hosts of war are sped,
They will find you, 'midst the quiet wondering faces
 Of the unnumbered dead.

"The Dead Lover" by John L C Brown

Were you quick and active once - you that lie so still?
Did your brain run nimbly once, your lungs expand and fill?
Were problems worth the trying, was the living worth the dying?
Did the flying moment pay you for the labour up the hill?

Ah, you stay so silent now! You could tell me why
Woods are green in April now, and men are made to die.
Do you feel the spring, I wonder, through the turf you're sleeping under,
Though the thunder and the sunshine cannot reach you where you lie?

The good rain trickles down to you and laps your limbs about,
The young grass has its roots in you, your bones and members sprout.
Ah, poor untimely lover, in new fashion you'll discover
The clover still is fragrant, and the primroses are out.

Though the old uneasy feeling cannot wake you sleeping there,
Nor the soft spring breezes dally with your crisp delightful hair,
Yet the flowers are round you clinging, and the dust about you springing,
And your singing spirit wanders like an essence in the air.

John L C Brown

"Rupert Brooke" 1887 - 1915

To have lived and loved - yea, even for a little,
  To have known the sun and fulness of the earth;
To have tasted joy nor stayed to prove it brittle,
  And travelled grief to find it end in mirth;
To have loved the good in life, and followed, groping,
  Beauty that lives among the common things,
Awaiting, eager-eyed and strongly hoping,
  The faint far beating of an angel's wings.

All these were his. And with his soul's releasing,
  Dearest of all, immortal youth has crowned him,
    And that bright spirit is young eternally;
Dreaming, he hears the great winds blow unceasing,
  And over him, about him, and around him,
    The music and the thunder of the sea.

John L C Brown

"**The Face**" by Frederick Manning

Out of the smoke of men's wrath,
The red mist of anger,
Suddenly,
As a wraith of sleep,
A boy's face, white and tense,
Convulsed with terror and hate,
The lips trembling...

GALLIPOLI

An Australian teacher, Gellert landed at Gallipoli, 25 April, 1915, in the first wave of the invasion, and suffered shrapnel, dysentery and blood poisoning. Invalided out, he was repatriated in 1916 and later became a journalist.

"**Anzac Cove**" by Leon Gellert.

There's a lonely stretch of hillocks:
  There's a beach asleep and drear:
There's a battered broken fort beside the sea.
There are sunken trampled graves:
  And a little rotting pier;
And winding paths that wind unceasingly.

There's a torn and silent valley:
  There's a tiny rivulet
With some blood upon the stones beside its mouth.
There are lines of buried bones:
  There's an unpaid waiting debt:
There's a sound of gentle sobbing in the South.

L Gellert

A.P. Herbert was an officer in the Royal Naval Division. At Gallipoli, in May 1915, before the third Battle of Krithia, he and his Oxford friend Lt. William Ker took a swimming party down to the Dardanelles, and he wrote this poem the same month.

"The Bathe"

Come friend and swim. We may be better then,
  But here the dust blows ever in the eyes
And wrangling round are weary fevered men,
  For ever mad with flies.
I cannot sleep, nor ever long lie still,
  And you have read your April paper twice;
To-morrow we must stagger up the hill
  To man a trench and live among the lice.

But yonder, where the Indians have their goats,
  There is a rock stands sheer above the blue,
Where one may sit and count the bustling boats
  And breathe the cool air through;
May find it still is good to be alive,
  May look across and see the Trojan shore
Twinkling and warm, may strip, and stretch, and dive, -
  And for a space forget about the war.

Then will we sit and talk of happy things,
  Home and 'The High' and some far fighting friend,
And gather strength for what the morrow brings,
  For that may be the end.
It may be we shall never swim again,
  Never be clean and comely to the sight,
May rot untombed and stink with all the slain,
  Come, then and swim. Come and be clean to-night.

A P Herbert

Patrick Shaw-Stewart, the most talented and brilliant man of his generation, Balliol scholar, First in Greats, Fellow of All Souls at 22, Managing Director of Barings Bank at 24. Volunteered, Sept 1914, and sailed for the Dardanelles in Feb 1915, as Lt. Commander i/c Hood Battalion. Shared rooms/cabins with friend Rupert Brooke (whom he later buried). Only known poem, written on Imbros, June 1915, in his copy of 'A Shropshire Lad'. Killed in France fighting with his old battalion, 30 December 1917.

"Achilles In The Trench"

I saw a man this morning
  Who did not wish to die:
I ask, and cannot answer,
  If otherwise wish I.

Fair broke the day this morning
  Upon the Dardanelles;
The breeze blew soft, the morn's cheeks
  Were cold as cold sea-shells.

But other shells are waiting
  Across the Aegean sea,
Shrapnel and high explosive,
  Shells and hells for me.

Oh hell of ships and cities,
  Hell of men like me,
Fatal second Helen,
  Why must I follow thee?

Achilles came to Troyland
  And I to Chersonese:
He turned from wrath to battle,
  And I from three days' peace.

Was it so hard Achilles,
So very hard to die?
Thou knowest and I know not -
So much the happier I.

I will go back this morning
From Imbros over the sea;
Stand in the trench, Achilles,
Flame-capped, and shout for me.
P Shaw-Stewart

"**Suvla Bay**" by W H Littlejohn
CSM in Middlesex Regiment, to Gallipoli 1915.

Old rose and black and indigo,
Saffron streaks in a spume-tipped grey,
Purple, laved in the dawn's wan glow -
God, how fair you are, Suvla Bay!

Spitting shrapnel and shrieking steel,
Brave men dead in their youth's noonday,
All the anguish their loved ones feel
Is your ambrose, fair Suvla Bay!

Stabbing sun from a brazen sky,
Choking dust from the corpse-strewn way,
Each one treads as he marches by,-
God, how I loathe you, Suvla Bay!

Tanned men delving with laboured breath,
Stinking lighters discharging hay,
Grey-hulled battleships belching death,
God, there's work on at Suvla Bay!

Pale, pale moon and the cold north star,
You who watch while I kneel and pray,
Take to her in the northland far
One sobbing prayer from Suvla Bay!

One sobbing prayer that the dull heart-pain
God in heav'n Thou alone canst stay,
For her be stilled till I come again
Back to her side from Suvla Bay!
W H Littlejohn

"Holy Communion Service, Suvla Bay"

Behold a table spread!
A battered corned-beef box, a length of twine,
An altar-rail of twigs and shreds of string.
. . . For the unseen, divine,
Uncomprehended Thing
A hallowed space amid the holy dead.

Behold a table spread!
And on a fair, white cloth the bread and wine,
The symbols of sublime compassioning,
The very outward sign
Of that the nations sing,
The body that He gave, the blood He shed.

Behold a table spread!
And kneeling soldiers in God's battle-line,
A line of homage to a mightier King:
All-knowing All-benign!
Hearing the prayers they bring,
Grant to them strength to follow where He led.

W H Littlejohn

"The Hospital Ship"

There is a green-lit hospital ship,
Green, with a crimson cross,
Lazily swaying there in the bay,
Lazily bearing my friend away,
Leaving me dull-sensed loss.
Green-lit, red-lit hospital ship,
Numb is my heart, but you carelessly dip
There in the drift of the bay.

There is a green-lit hospital ship,
Dim as the distance grows,
Speedily steaming out of the bay,
Speedily bearing my friend away
Into the orange-rose.
Green-lit, red-lit hospital ship,
Dim are my eyes, but you heedlessly slip
Out of their sight from the bay.

There was a green-lit hospital ship,
Green, with a blood-red cross,
Lazily swaying there in the bay,
But it went out with the light of the day -
Out where the white seas toss.
Green-lit, red-lit hospital ship,
Cold are my hands and trembling my lip:
Did you make home from the bay?

W H Littlejohn

"The Turkish Trench Dog" by Geoffrey Dearmer

Dearmer's family all served in the Gallipoli campaign: his father was a Chaplain, his mother a red cross paramedic, who died in Serbia, and his younger brother, a pilot with the RNAS, was killed in action there in October 1915. Geoffrey, in the Royal Fusiliers, lived to be 103!

A surprising night encounter in No Man's Land at Gallipoli.

Night held me as I crawled and scrambled near
The Turkish lines. Above, the mocking stars
Silvered the curving parapet, and clear
Cloud-latticed beams o'erflecked the land with bars;
I, crouching, lay between
Tense-listening armies peering through the night,
Twin giants bound by tentacles unseen.
Here in dim-shadowed light
I saw him, as a sudden movement turned
His eyes towards me, glowing eyes that burned
A moment ere his snuffling muzzle found
My trail; and then as serpents mesmerize,
He chained me with those unrelenting eyes,
That muscle-sliding rhythm, knit and bound
In spare-limbed symmetry, those perfect jaws
And soft-approaching pitter-patter paws.
Nearer and nearer like a wolf he crept -
That moment had my swift revolver leapt -
But terror seized me, terror born of shame
Brought flooding revelation. For he came
As one who offers comradeship deserved,
An open ally of the human race,
And sniffling at my prostrate form unnerved,
He licked my face!

G Dearmer - 1915

Aubrey Herbert, Eton and Balliol, son of an earl, was barred from service by his awful eyesight, but as a gifted linguist became liaison officer and interpreter during the Gallipoli campaign of 1915, and then helped to secure Albania's independence. He was also an MP 1911-1923.

"Ode to a Young Man" - "R B" by Aubrey Herbert

It was April we left Lemnos, shining sea and snow-white camp,
Passing onward into darkness. Lemnos shone a golden lamp,
As a low harp tells of thunder, so the lovely Lemnos air
Whispered of the dawn and battle; and we left a comrade there.
He who sang of dawn and evening, English glades and light of Greece,
Changed his dreaming into sleeping, left his sword to rest in peace.
Left his visions of the springtime, Holy Grail and Golden Fleece,
Took the leave that has no ending, till the waves of Lemnos cease.
There will be enough recorders ere this fight of ours be done,
And the deeds of men made little, swiftly cheapened one by one;
Bitter loss his golden harpstrings and the treasure of his youth;
Gallant foe and friend may mourn him, for he sang the knightly truth.
Joy was his in his clear singing, clean as is the swimmer's joy;
Strong the wine he drank of battle, fierce as that they poured in Troy.
Swift the shadows steal from Athos, but his soul was morning-swift,
Greek and English he made music, caught the cloud thoughts we let drift.
Sleep you well, you rainbow comrade, where the wind and light is strong,
Overhead and high above you, let the lark take up your song.
Something of your singing lingers, for the men like me who pass,
Till all singing ends in sighing, in the sighing of the grass.

A second tribute to dead friend Rupert Brooke

"To R - at Anzac"

You left your vineyards, dreaming of the vines in a dream land
And dim Italian cities where high cathedrals stand.
At Anzac in the evening, so many things we planned,
And now you sleep with comrades in the Anafarta sand.

There are men go gay to battle like the cavaliers to dance,
And some with happy dreamings like princes in romance,
And some men march unquestioning to where the answer lies,
The dawn that comes like darkness they meet with lover's eyes.

You heard the bugles call to arms, and like a storm men's cheers,
But veiled behind that music, you knew the women's tears.
You heard the Vikings singing in a rapture to the sea,
And passing clear beyond that song, the waves of Galilee.

You lived for peace and lived for war, you knew no little strife;
To conquer first, then help your foe, made music of your life.
And for the sake of those you led, you gave your life away,
As youth might fling a coin of gold upon a sunny day.

If Odin mustered Vikings, you would rule his pagan crew.
If Mary came to choose her knights, she'd hand her sword to you.
Men scattered in the wilderness, or crowded in the street,
Would choose you for their leader and glory in defeat.

You'd find a bridge to Lazarus, or any man in pain.
There are not many like you that I shall see again;
I do not grieve for you who laughed, and went into the shade,
I sorrow for the dream that's lost, Italian plans we made.

Good-bye! It's Armageddon. You will not prune your vine,
Nor taste the salt of channel winds, nor hear the singing Rhine.
You'll sleep with friends and enemies until the trumpet sounds,
And open are the thrones of kings, and all the Trojan mounds.

When women's tears arc rainbows then, that shine across the sky,
And swords are raised in last salute, to a comrade enemy,
And what men fought and failed for, or what men strove and won,
Are like forgotten shadows, and clouds that hid the sun.

Aubrey Herbert

Frederick W D Bendall, a teacher at Bridlington Grammar School, after a scholarship to Selwyn, Cambridge, was promoted from Captain to Lieutenant Colonel in September 1914 i/c the London Regt. He sailed to Egypt in 1915, where he wrote this first of his war poems, waiting to sail north to Gallipoli:

I see the birds go North
Go North across the sea
And with them winging free
I feel my heart fly forth;
The swallow on the eaves
Of that dear Northland, soon
Will trill his tiny tune
To waking buds and leaves;
The nightingale will bring
Within her golden mouth
A love song from the South
To charm the ears of Spring.
And you will hear them all
And as each treble flute

Awakes the woodland mute
Perchance a whispered call
Will touch your hearing too
With music-laden wings;
It is my heart that sings
The Song of Songs for you.
F Bendall

"The Blizzard"

27 November 1915, a great flood drowned all but 45 of Bendall's brigade of 500 at Suvla; he was evacuated to hospital in Alexandria, then England.

The night was dark as hell-mouth the wind was bitter cold,
And there was little comfort in a sodden blanket rolled.
A foot or two of water - an inch or two of mud -
Was what we had to walk in before came down - the flood
It caught the shivering sentries along the parapet,
The front trench was abrim before they knew that they were wet,
Full seven feet deep the trenches were, the men were weighted down
With kit and ammunition, and mostly had to drown.
Behind was soon no better – a million tons of rain
Came flooding thro' the section by dug out, sap and drain.
Headquarters, store and cook-house, bomb-shelter, splinter-proof,
Were all filled up with water, and in fell every roof.
Scummy and dark and icy, the torrent at a touch
Sucked in the greasy trench-walls that mocked the drowning clutch.
And now, the land was covered, and now with choking breath
The wretched victims unawares stepped into hidden death.
Behind the up-flung parados – half buried in the slime,
Their fingers numb and useless – their rifles choked with grime,
Thro' thirty hours of darkness and twenty hours of day,
Foodless and drinkless (save the mark) a frozen handful lay.
My friends at home - at breakfast, you saw a casual hint,
Of half a quarter of the truth in seven lines of print.
But from the sullen skies above that seemed to mock our woes
God saw my soldiers freeze and drown. It is enough. He knows.
by F W D Bendall

"Suvla Bay"

Bendall at Gallipoli, 27 September - 6 December, 1915.

In silhouettes of silver and of gray,
With tall fantastic peaks against the sky
Of crimson and saffron in the dying day,
Imbros and Samothrace to westward lie.
No seabirds homing to the salt lake fly
Across the sapphire waters of the bay,
But thunder-echoes roll and faint and die
As the lean warship seeks her distant prey.
Yet not to westward in the sunset's fire
Our eyes are set, tho' there a splendour burns.
Nay-eastward - where the morning light comes in
The grave of hope - the death-place of desire -
The goal to which each ardent spirit yearns,
The sombre-circled heights we could not win.

F W D Bendall

HUMOUR

William Kersley Holmes a banker, 32 when war broke out, Holmes joined a Scottish cavalry regiment as a Lance-corporal, then, fighting in France, transferred to the Artillery as an officer. His light touch and humour make him easily accessible. He published two volumes of popular poems in 1915: 'Ballads of Field and Billet', and 'More Ballads...' including the following two poems:

"The Soldier Mood"

The comfort of eating chips with their fingers provides a welcome escape from the threat of unknown terrors, followed by a song, probably "It's a Long Way to Tipperary"!

We were eating chip potatoes underneath the April stars
That glittered coldly and aloof from earth and earthly wars;
We were three good pals together and the day's hard work was done,
So we munched our chip potatoes, half for food and half for fun.

Half the world was war's dominion, but the matter of the strife
Had come to seem accustomed as the undertone of life;
We were fit and hard and happy, and the future was unknown,
The past - all put behind us; but the present was our own.

We were doing our plainest duty, meant to end what we'd begun;
Why worry for to-morrow till to-day's big job was done?
So we walked and laughed together like three modern musketeers -
Defying indigestion and the Germans and the years.

We were eating chip potatoes with our fingers, like a tramp,
And the unseen owls were hooting in the trees around the camp;
We were happy to be hungry, glad to be alive and strong;
So - to-morrow might be terror, but tonight could be a song!

W K Holmes

"Singing Tipperary" - a Global hit, August 1914

We've each our Tipperary who shout that haunting song,
And all the more worth reaching because the way is long;
You'll hear the hackneyed chorus until it tires your brain
Unless you feel the thousand hopes disguised in that refrain.

We've each our Tipperary - some hamlet, village, town,
To which our ghosts would hasten though we laid our bodies down,
Some spot of little showing our spirits still would seek,
And strive, unseen, to utter what now we fear to speak.

We've each our Tipperary, our labour to inspire,
Some mountain-top or haven, some goal of far desire -
Some old forlorn ambition, or humble, happy hope
That shines beyond the doubting with which our spirits cope.

We've each our Tipperary - near by or wildly far;
For some it means a fireside, for some it means a star;
For some it's but a journey by homely roads they know,
For some a spirit's venture where none but theirs may go.

We've each our Tipperary, where rest and love and peace
Mean just a mortal maiden, or Dante's Beatrice;
We growl a song together, to keep the marching swing,
But who shall dare interpret the chorus that we sing?

W K Holmes

1898-1915 saw the flourishing of "Ragtime", with the 'Hop' 'Slide' 'Trot' & 'Glide' etc: epitomised by Scott Joplin. Sivori Levey composed a rare "Ragtime" War Poem.

Sivori Levey was born Steyning, Sussex in 1879; a composer, actor and pianist, he was blown into a shell hole at Ypres by a mortar, where he wrote this poem and composed its music; it was performed at many Regimental concerts in WWI. Later he lost a leg at Passchendaele, but survived the war.

"The Duck Board"

It's a long way to Tipperary,
Or so it always seems;
There'a a long, long trail awinding
Into the land of dreams.
And there's a long and narrow path
Our Warriors know well,
For one way leads to Blighty,
And the other one to - well!

Chorus
It's the Duck Board Glide,
It's the Duck Board Slide
On a cold and frosty night;
For it's over a mile
In single file
Out in the pale moon-light.
It's nippy; slippy
Bumpy; jumpy
Shell-holes either side;

And when machine guns cough
You can all drop off
That Duck Board Glide.

It's very dark and lonely,
  And you see, when on the top,
A Very Light; so in the trench
  You very lightly drop.
But when you want to reach the line,
  That's done as best you may,
There's only one path that you have to take,
  It is the only way.

Chorus: It's the Duck Board Glide,
              It's the Duck Board Slide...

When you were young and went to Church,
  Or chapel, it may be,
The Padre use to take some text
  To strafe you all with glee.
"The path is long and narrow
  Along which you ought to go!"
We did not know then what it was,
  But now of course, we know.

Chorus: It's the Duck Board Glide,
              It's the Duck Board Slide...

Sivori Levey

Printed in the British Expeditionary Force's Trench Paper on Christmas Day 1917, yet another Ragtime Poem (Anon.) but, like Levey's "Duck Board", by another Englishman, the year before Wyeth's songs:-

"Why Not?"

We've had a play in ragtime, and we've had a ragtime band,
We've had a ragtime army, and we've had a ragtime land;
But why not let us have what we've never had before?
Let's wade right in tomorrow and let's have a ragtime war.
Let's carry up our duckboards to a ragtime's jerky strains,
Let's whistle ragtime ditties while we're bashing out Hun brains,
Let's introduce this melody in all we say or do,
In our operation orders, and in all our lies to Q.
Let us write O.O.s to music, and the red-hats can decide
The witching hour of zero to a dainty Gaby Glide;

We'll take the fateful plunge, and when we venture o'er the top
We'll do it to a Turkey Trot or tuneful Boston Hop.
We'll drink our S.R.D. to tune, and even 'chatting up'
Becomes a melody in rhyme if done to 'Dixie Pup',
A bombing raid to 'Old Kentuck' would make a Fritzie smile,
He'd stop a bomb with pleasure to a ragtime's mystic guile.
Can you see our giddy 'Q' staff, as they go up the line,
Just walking round the trenches to the air 'Kentucky Mine',
Gaily prancing down the duckboards, as they tumble o'er a bucket
To the quiet seducing strains of 'My Dear Home in Old Kentucket'.

Anon.

R B Glaenzer has fun with his mocking irony:

"Sure, It's Fun - What fun to be a soldier! - Everykid"

Sure, it's fun to be a soldier! Oh, it's fun, fun, fun,
Upon an iron shoulder-blade to tote a feather gun;
To hike with other brave galoots in easy-going army-boots;
To pack along a one-ounce sack, the commissary on your track;
To tramp, tramp, tramp, to a right-and-ready camp!
Fun? - Sure, it's fun, just the finest ever, son!

Yes, it's fun to be a soldier! Oh, it's fun, fun, fun,
To loaf along a level road beneath a cloudless sun
Or over fields of golden grain, kept cool by puffs of wind and rain;
Then richly, more-than-fully, fed, to stretch upon a downy bed
And sleep, sleep, sleep, while the stay-at-homes weep!
Fun? - Sure, it's fun, just the finest ever, son!

Oh, it's fun to be a soldier! Oh, it's fun, fun, fun,
To catch the silly enemy and get 'em on the run;
To here and there blow off a head with just a bit of chuckling lead;
To bayonet a foolish bloke at hide-and-seek in trench and smoke;
To shoot, shoot, shoot, till they've got no legs to scoot!
Fun? - Sure, it's fun, just the finest ever, son!

God, it's fun to be a soldier! Oh, it's fun, fun, fun
To lie out still and easy when your day's sport's done;
With not a thing to worry for, nor anything to hurry for;
Not hungry, thirsty, tired, but a hero much-admired;
Just dead, dead, dead, like Jack and Bill and Fred!
Fun? - Sure, it's fun, just the finest ever, son!

Richard Butler Glaenzer

"Elegy on the Death of Bingo, Our Trench Dog"

Weep, weep, ye dwellers in the delvèd earth,
Ah, weep, ye watchers by the dismal shore
Of No Man's land, for Bingo is no more;
He is no more, and well ye knew his worth,
For whom on bully-beefless days were kept
Rare bones by each according to his means,
And, while the Quartermaster-Sergeant slept,
The elusive pork was rescued from the beans.
He is no more, and, impudently brave,
The loathly rats sit grinning on his grave.

Him mourn the grimy cooks and bombers ten,
The sentinels in lonely posts forlorn,
The fierce patrols with hands and tunics torn,
The furtive band of sanitary men.
The murmuring sound of grief along the length
Of traversed trench the startled Hun could hear;
The captain, as he struck him off the strength,
Let fall a sad and solitary tear;
'Tis even said a batman passing by
Had seen the Sergeant-Major wipe his eye.

The fearful fervour of the feline chase
He never knew, poor dog, he never knew;
Content with optimistic zeal to woo
Reluctant rodents in this murky place,
He never played with children on clean grass,
Nor dozed at ease beside the glowing embers,
Nor watched with hopeful eye the tea-cakes pass,
Nor smelt the heather-smell of Scotch Septembers,
For he was born amid a world at war
Although unrecking what we struggled for.

Yet who shall say that Bingo was unblest
Though all his Spratless life was passed beneath
The roar of mortars and the whistling breath
Of grim, nocturnal heavies going west?
Unmoved he heard the evening hymn of hate,
Unmoved would gaze into his master's eyes.
For all the sorrows men for men create
In search of happiness wise dogs despise,
Finding ecstatic joy in every rag
And every smile of friendship worth a wag.

Edward de Stein

"Lieutenant Tattoon M.C." by Edward Carpenter
(substitute 's' for 't' above!) - Nov. 1917

The case of Lieutenant Tattoon, M.C.
  Is worthy of some remark.
He thought (and one should not think, you see)
That the War which was to make people free
  Was now being fought in the dark.

For at first (he said) our aims were clear,
  Men gave their lives with gladness
To save small nations from the fear
Of Tyrants who would domineer
  And doom mankind to madness.

Our rulers had claimed - and rightly I ween -
  That the Germans must be 'broken';
But afterwards, What that word might mean,
And what sort of peace was to supervene,
  Were things which they left unspoken.

And no one knew whatever on Earth
  Our present objective and aim were,
And whether the loss and deadly dearth
Of another Million lives was worth
  Some gains in Mesopotamia.

These were the thoughts of Lieutenant Tattoon -
  Of course it was very improper,
But he actually gave them expression, and soon
Found out he was trying to jump the Moon
  And only coming a cropper!

For to say what you mean is all right as a rule
  In a far overseas Dominion,
But at home or under the Prussian school
It is not safe - and a man is a fool
  Even to have an opinion.

A Medical Borad sat on him, in state
  (No wonder they looked so solemn);
His sins were entered upon the slate
With every lapse detailed to date -
  And they added up the Column.

'Twas insubordination, they said,
  And he surely must be crazy -
Yet there he stood, in mien well-bred,
Collected and calm, with a clean-cut head,
  And looking as fit as a daisy.

An M.C. too - so what could they do?
  'Twas a most provoking and strange craze.
Yet to put him in prison a storm would brew
Of wrath - the mere proposal to mew
  A hero in Woking or Strangeways!

For half an hour (as once in Heaven)
  Silence fell on the folk assembled;
Till by one inspired the stillness was riven:
'Twas nervous shock'. The cue was given -
  And the whole Court gaily dissembled.

'Poor fellow!' they cried, ' 'Twas nervous strain,
  He's a subject for our pity;
Let him to Hospital go, till his brain
Is healed, and there's no danger again
  That he will repeat that ditty.'

To a Shell-shock ward he then was sent,
  And there he was kindly treated
And even indulged to the top of his bent; -
But there ever since he has safely been pent,
  And his words have not been repeated.

Edward Carpenter

Very accurate Sassoon was still in Craiglockhart Hospital, Edinburgh, when this poem published, in November 1917!

Edgell Rickword joined the Artist Rifles as soon as he became 18, in 1916, won the MC and wrote war poetry. In 1919 he lost an eye through septicaemia, then went up to Oxford, but left after four terms to get married. He wrote for literary reviews and became a leading Communist during the 1930-40s.

"Trench Poets" by Edgell Rickword

I knew a man, he was my chum,
But he grew blacker every day,
And would not brush the flies away,
Nor blanch however fierce the hum
Of passing shells; I used to read,
To rouse him, random things from Donne;
Like "Get with child a mandrake-root,"
But you can tell he was far gone,
For he lay gaping, mackerel-eyed,
And stiff and senseless as a post
Even when that old poet cried
"I long to talk with some old lover's ghost."
I tried the Elegies one day,
But he, because he heard me say
"What needst thou have more covering than a man?"
Grinned nastily, and so I knew
The worms had got his brains at last.
There was one thing that I might do
To starve the worms; I racked my head
For healthy things and quoted "Maud."
His grin got worse and I could see
He laughed at passion's purity.
He stank so badly, though we were great chums
I had to leave him; then rats ate his thumbs.

"Winter Warfare" by Edgell Rickword

Colonel Cold strode up the Line
  (tabs of rime and spurs of ice);
stiffened all that met his glare:
  horses, men and lice.

Visited a forward post,
  left them burning, ear to foot;
fingers stuck to biting steel,
  toes to frozen boot.

Stalked on into No Man's Land,
  turned the wire to fleecy wool,
iron stakes to sugar sticks
  snapping at a pull.

Those who watched with hoary eyes
  saw two figures gleaming there;
Hauptmann Kälte, colonel old,
  gaunt in the grey air.

Stiffly, tinkling spurs they moved,
  glassy-eyed, with glinting heel
stabbing those who lingered there
  torn by screaming steel.

"Bill The Bomber" by Robert Service

The poppies gleamed like bloody pools through cotton-woolly mist;
The Captain kept a-lookin' at the watch upon his wrist;
And there we smoked and squatted, as we watched the shrapnel flame;
'Twas wonnerful, I'm tellin' you, how fast them bullets came.
'Twas weary work the waiting, though; I tried to sleep a wink,
For waitin' means a-thinkin', and it doesn't do to think.
So I closed my eyes a little, and I had a niceish dream
Of a-standin' by a dresser with a dish of Devon cream;
But I hadn't time to sample it, for suddenlike I woke:
"Come on, me lads!" the Captain says, 'n I climbed out through the smoke.

We spread out in the open: it was like a bath of lead;
But the boys they cheered and hollered fit to raise the bloody dead,
Till a beastly bullet copped 'em, then they lay without a sound,
And it's odd -- we didn't seem to heed them corpses on the ground.
And I kept on thinkin', thinkin', as the bullets faster flew,
How they picks the werry best men, and they lets the rotters through;
So indiscriminatin' like, they spares a man of sin,
And a rare lad wot's a husband and a father gets done in.
And while havin' these reflections and advancin' on the run,
A bullet biffs me shoulder, and says I: "That's number one."

R Service

"Going Home" by Robert Service

I'm goin' 'ome to Blighty -- ain't I glad to 'ave the chance!
I'm loaded up wiv fightin', and I've 'ad my fill o' France;
I'm feelin' so excited-like, I want to sing and dance,
For I'm goin' 'ome to Blighty in the mawnin'.

I'm goin' 'ome to Blighty: can you wonder as I'm gay?
I've got a wound I wouldn't sell for 'alf a year o' pay;
A harm that's mashed to jelly in the nicest sort o' way,
For it takes me 'ome to Blighty in the mawnin'.

'Ow everlastin' keen I was on gettin' to the front!
I'd ginger for a dozen, and I 'elped to bear the brunt;
But Cheese and Crust! I'm crazy, now I've done me little stunt,
To sniff the air of Blighty in the mawnin'.

I've looked upon the wine that's white, and on the wine that's red;
I've looked on cider flowin', till it fairly turned me 'ead;
But oh, the finest scoff will be, when all is done and said,
A pint o' Bass in Blighty in the mawnin'.

I'm goin' back to Blighty, which I left to strafe the 'Un;
I've fought in bloody battles, and I've 'ad a 'eap of fun;
But now me flipper's busted, and I think me dooty's done,
And I'll kiss me gel in Blighty in the mawnin'.

Oh, there be furrin' lands to see, and some of 'em be fine;
And there be furrin' gels to kiss, and scented furrin' wine;
But there's no land like England, and no other gel like mine:
Thank Gawd for dear old Blighty in the mawnin'.

R Service

In 1913 Robert Service moved to Paris, married a French girl, Germaine, and settled there. In his next poem he includes some classic "franglais"!

"Tipperary Days" - 1914

Oh, weren't they the fine boys! You never saw the beat of them,
Singing all together with their throats bronze-bare;
Fighting-fit and mirth-mad, music in the feet of them,
Swinging on to glory and the wrath out there.

Laughing by and chaffing by, frolic in the smiles of them,
On the road, the white road, all the afternoon;
Strangers in a strange land, miles and miles and miles of them,
Battle-bound and heart-high, and singing this tune:

> It's a long way to Tipperary,
> It's a long way to go;
> It's a long way to Tipperary,
> And the sweetest girl I know.
> Goodbye, Piccadilly,
> Farewell Leicester Square:
> It's a long, long way to Tipperary,
> But my heart's right there.

Come Yvonne and Juliette! Come Mimi and cheer for them!
Throw them flowers and kisses as they pass you by.
Aren't they the lovely lads! Haven't you a tear for them,
Going out so gallantly to dare and die?

What is it they're singing so? Some high hymn of Motherland?
Some immortal chanson of their Faith and King?
Marseillaise or Brabancon, anthem of that other land,
Dears, let us remember it, that song they sing:

> C'est un chemin long 'to Tepararee',
> C'est un chemin long, c'est vrai;
> C'est un chemin long 'to Tepararee',
> Et la belle fille qu'je connais;
> Bonjour, Peekadeely!
> Au revoir, Lestaire Squaire!
> C'est un chemin long 'to Tepararee',
> Mais mon coeur 'ees zaire'.

The gallant 'Old Contemptibles'! There isn't much remains of them,
So full of fun and fitness, and a-singing in their pride;
For some are cold as clabber and the corby picks the brains of them,
And some are back in Blighty, and a-wishing they had died.
Ah me! It seems but yesterday, that great glad sight of them,

Swinging on to battle as the sky grew black and black;
Yet oh, their glee and glory, and the great, grim fight of them! —
Just whistle Tipperary and it all comes back:

It's a long way to Tipperary
(Which means 'ome anywhere);
It's a long way to Tipperary
(And the things wot make you care).
Goodbye, Piccadilly,
('Ow I 'opes my folks is well);
It's a long, long way to Tipperary —
('R! Aint war just 'ell?)

Robert Service

Humour from Cpt. Hugh Smith, a "letter" from the Front, to a Friend

"The Incorrigibles"

Keen through the shell-hole in my billet walls
The sad, dirge-laden wind of Flanders calls
(Hark! ere the words are written, have replied
The rumblings of my supperless inside!)
Keen (as I think I said) the north wind bellows,
And makes me envy all you lucky fellows
Who quaff at ease your bitters and your gin
Before you put your grill-room dinners in. —

Spake one to me and prated how that all
In war was Glory, Triumph and Trumpet-call;
And said that Death, who stalked across the field,
But sowed, that Life a nobler crop might yield!
Poor Vapourer! for now I know that he
Was on the Staff or in the A.S.C.
And in a well-manured hot-bed grew —
The ginger-bread is gilded but for few!
For us, foot-slogging sadly, it is clear
That War is fleas, short rations, watered beer,
Noise and mismanagement, bluster and foreboding,
Triumph but the sequel to enough exploding.
Yet a ray across the storm-torn sea
Shines through it all the glint of Comedy,
And pompous Death, whose table they have messed at,
Has given the Men another butt to jest at!

Hugh Stewart Smith

"**Plains Of Picardy**" by Cpt. Hugh S Smith

K.I.A. High Wood, 18 August 1916. Found in his diary:

On the plains of Picardy
Lay a soldier, dying
Gallantly, with soul still free
Spite the rough world's trying.
Came the angel who keeps guard
When the fight has drifted,
"What would you for your reward
When the Clouds have lifted?"
Then the soldier through the mist
Heard the voice and rested
As a man who sees his home
When the hill is breasted —
This his answer and I vow
Nothing could be fitter —
Give me Peace, a dog, a friend
And a glass of bitter.

LEGACY - PEACE, HOPE & DIPLOMACY

"Bach and the Sentry"

Watching the dark my spirit rose in flood
On that most dearest Prelude of my delight.
The low-lying mist lifted its hood,
The October stars shewed nobly in clear night.
When I return, and to real music-making,
And play that Prelude, how will it happen then?
Shall I feel as I felt, a sentry hardly waking,
With a dull sense of No Man's Land again?

Ivor Gurney 8 November 1916

"Soldier's Dream" by Wilfred Owen

I dreamed kind Jesus fouled the big-gun gears;
And caused a permanent stoppage in all bolts;
And buckled with a smile Mausers and Colts;
And rusted every bayonet with His tears.

And there were no more bombs, of ours or Theirs,
Not even an old flint-lock, nor even a pikel.
But God was vexed, and gave all power to Michael;
And when I woke he'd seen to our repairs.

"May 1915" by Charlotte Mew

Let us remember Spring will come again
To the scorched, blackened woods, where the wounded trees
Wait, with their old wise patience for the heavenly rain,
Sure of the sky; sure of the sea to send its healing breeze,
Sure of the sun.
And even as to these
Surely the Spring, when God shall please,
Will come again like a divine surprise
To those who sit to-day with their great dead, hands in their hands, eyes in their eyes,
At one with Love, at one with Grief: blind to the scattered things and changing skies.

"Since They Have Died" by May Wedderburn Cannan

Since they have died to give us gentleness,
And hearts kind with contentment and quiet mirth,
Let us who live give also happiness
And love, that's born of pity, to the earth.
For, I have thought, some day they may lie sleeping
Forgetting all the weariness and pain,
And smile to think their world is in our keeping,
And laughter come back to the earth again.
February 1916

LHB was Leslie Beauchamp, Catherine's younger brother; they were raised together in New Zealand. In October 1915, Leslie was killed during a grenade training drill near Ypres. Next year this poem came to Mansfield in a dream:

"To L.H.B. (1894-1915)" by Catherine Mansfield, 1916

Last night for the first time since you were dead
I walked with you, my brother, in a dream.
We were at home again beside the stream
Fringed with tall berry bushes, white and red.
"Don't touch them; they are poisonous," I said.
But your hand hovered, and I saw a beam
Of strange, bright laughter flying round your head
And as you stooped I saw the berries gleam.
"Don't you remember? We called them Dead Man's Bread!"
I woke and heard the wind moan and the roar
Of the dark water tumbling on the shore.
Where - where is the path of my dream for my eager feet?
By the remembered stream my brother stands
Waiting for me with berries in his hands ...
"These are my body. Sister, take and eat."

"Women Demobilized" by May Cannan

Now must we go again back to the world
Full of grey ghosts and voices of men dying,
And in the rain the sounding of last posts,
And Lovers' crying —
Back to the old, back to the empty world.

Now are put by the bugles and the drums,
And the worn spurs, and the great swords they carried,

Now are we made most lonely, proudly, theirs,
The men we married:
Under the dome the long roll of the drums.
Now are the Fallen happy and sleep sound,
Now, in the end, to us is come the paying,
These who return will find the love they spend,
But we are praying
Love of our Lovers fallen who sleep sound.
Now in our hearts abides always our war,
Time brings, to us, no day for our forgetting,
Never for us is folded War away,
Dawn or sun setting,
Now in our hearts abides always our war.
May Cannan - July 1919

"An Die Soldaten Des Grossen Krieges"
- "To The Soldiers Of The Great War"
by Gerrit Engelke (4 of the 9 verses)

"No people hates the other, it is the powerful speculators without a conscience who manage the war." *Wounded 11 October 1918, rescued by the British next day, but died a day later, in a British Field Hospital.*

Rise up! Out of trenches, muddy holes, concrete bunkers, quarries.
Up out of mud and fire, chalk dust and stench of corpses!
Come along! Comrades! For from front to front, from battlefield to battlefield,
May the world's new red-letter day come to you all!
Off with your steel helmets, caps, képis! And away with your rifles!
Enough of this bloody enmity and murderous sense of honour.

You all I implore by your country's villages and towns
To stamp out, to weed out the monstrous seeds of hatred,
Implore you by the love of your sisters, mothers, children,
Which alone still disposes your scarred heart to sing.
By the love of your wife — I too love a woman!
By the love of your mother — a mother's body bore me too!
By your love of your child — for I love little ones!
And the houses are full of cursing, praying, weeping!

Oh, that brother may again really be called brother!
That east and west may recognise the same values!
That joy may again flash into all nations,
And man be roused to goodness by man!

From front to front and battlefield to battlefield,
Let us sing the birthday of the new world!
Out of every chest let a single tune ring forth:
The psalm of peace, of reconciliation, of revolt!
And may the surging, radiant song,
The thrilling, brother-embracing,
The wild and divinely compassionate song
Of thousandfold love ring out around the earth!

Alec de Candole, son of a priest and intending to follow his father into the Church, postponed his Cambridge scholarship and enlisted as soon as he left Marlborough in 1916, three years after Sorley, and wrote this while training:

"**War**" - November 4th, 1916.

We never dreamed that war would come again,
That we should see men fight round windy Troy,
That we ourselves should feel the battle-joy,
That we should know ourselves the battle-pain.

We read of all the wounds and toil and heat,
Of noble acts, and mighty deeds of fame,

The building up of many a glorious name;
But, far away, 'twas bitterness grown sweet.

And now ourselves we plunge beneath its wave,
And feel the loss; and yet with purpose sure
All things, to save the world, we can endure:
-They save the world; themselves they cannot save.

But those who found thus nobly with their blood
A newer world, and those whose harder call
'Twill be to build it true, alike we all
Work in one hope and trust one boundless God.

Candole was killed during a bombing raid near Aubigny, north-west of Arras, 3 September 1918. His final poem, untitled, written the day before he died, looks forward to returning home when peace is restored — which lay two months ahead:

When the last long trek is over,
And the last long trench filled in,
I'll take a boat to Dover,
Away from all the din;
I'll take a trip to Mendip,
I'll see the Wilshire downs,

And all my soul I'll then dip
In peace no trouble drowns.

Away from noise of battle,
Away from bombs and shells,
I'll lie where browse the cattle,
Or pluck the purple bells.
I'll lie among the heather,
And watch the distant plain,
Through all the summer weather,
Nor go to fight again.

Alec de Candole, 2 September 1918

Like Edward Thomas, Robert Vernède was educated at St.Paul's School, and then Oxford. He was also killed on the same day, 9 April 1917, aged nearly 42. Enlisting, over-age, in 1915-16 he fought in the Ypres Salient and then on the Somme, where he was wounded in the thigh.

"**To Our Fallen**" by Robert Ernest Vernède

Ye Sleepers, who will sing you?
We can but give our tears --
Ye dead men, who shall bring you
Fame in the coming years?
Brave souls . . . but who remembers
The flame that fired your embers? . . .
Deep, deep the sleep that holds you
Who one time had no peers.

Yet maybe Fame's but seeming
And praise you'd set aside,
Content to go on dreaming,
Yea, happy to have died
If of all things you prayed for --
All things your valour paid for --
One prayer is not forgotten,
One purchase not denied.

But God grants your dear England
A strength that shall not cease
Till she have won for all the Earth
From ruthless men release,
And made supreme upon her
Mercy and Truth and Honour --
Is this the thing you died for?
Oh, Brothers, sleep in peace!

December 1914

"How Long, O Lord?"

How Long, O Lord, how long, before the flood
Of crimson-welling carnage shall abate?
From sodden plains in West and East the blood
Of kindly men streams up in mists of hate,
Polluting Thy clean air: and nations great
In reputation of the arts that bind
The world with hopes of Heaven, sink to the state
Of brute barbarians, whose ferocious mind
Gloats o'er the bloody havoc of their kind,
Not knowing love or mercy. Lord, how long
Shall Satan in high places lead the blind
To battle for the passions of the strong?
Oh, touch Thy children's hearts, that they may know
Hate their most hateful, pride their deadliest foe.

R. E. Vernède

The first Christmas Truce of 1914 was suppressed by the General Staff, and Ewer predicts that they will forestall it again.

"Christmas Truce"

In France, maybe, war-weary men,
Thinking once more of home and peace,
Will bid this daily horror cease,
And call the truce of God again.
Will meet their enemy, and call
Him friend, and take him by the hand,
And, for the moment understand,
The bloody folly of it all.

But while in Flanders foe is friend,
Far from the shell-scarred battle-line
Old men will sit and sip their wine,
And talk about 'the bitter end'.
And reckon up the tale of dead,
And hate the foe they never saw,
And vow to carry on the war
Till the last drop of bleed be shed.

So will they stop the truce of Christ,
Will bid the battle re-begin;
And for the Elder Statesmen's sin
More young lives shall be sacrificed.

W. N. Ewer

W N Ewer castigates the imperial rivalries that led to WWI:

"To Any Diplomatist"

Heading nought else, your subtle game you played,
Took tricks and lost them, reckoned up the score,
Balanced defeats with triumphs, less with more,
And plotted how the next point might be made:

How some sly move with counter moves to meet,
How by some crafty stratagem to gain
This empty point of honour, how obtain
That barren symbol of a foe's defeat.

Engrossed, you never cared to realise
The folly of the things for which you fought,
The hideous peril which your striving brought —
A witless struggle for a worthless prize!
God! Were you fiends or fools, who, in your game,
Heedless, have set the circling earth aflame?

February 1916

Ewer suspects Britain plans to take over German colonies.

"No Annexations"

"No annexations?" We agree!
 We did not draw the sword for gain,
But to keep little nations free;
 And surely, surely, it is plain
 That land and loot we must disdain,
Who only fight for liberty.

But, still — we cannot well restore
 To the grim teuton's iron yoke
The countries that he ruled before,
 Rebind on liberated folk
 The cruel fetters that we broke,
The grievous burden that they bore.

Of course it happens — as we know —
 That 'German East' has fertile soil
Where corn and cotton crops will grow,
 That Togoland is rich in oil,
 That natives can be made to toil
For wages white men count too low.

That many a wealthy diamond mine
 Makes South-West Africa a prize,
That river-dam and railway line
 (A profitable enterprise)
 May make a paying paradise
Of Bagdad and of Palestine.

However, this is by the way;
 We do not fight for things like these
But to destroy a despot's sway,
 To guard our ancient liberties:
 We cannot help it if it please
The Gods to make the process pay.

We cannot help it if our Fate
 Decree that war in Freedom's name
Shall handsomely remunerate
 Our ruling classes. 'Twas the same
 In earlier days — we always came
Not to annex, but liberate.

W N Ewer, 1918

"War and Peace"

In sodden trenches I have heard men speak,
Though numb and wretched, wise and witty things;
And loved them for the stubbornness that clings
Longest to laughter when Death's pulleys creak;

And seeing cool nurses move on tireless feet
To do abominable things with grace,
Deemed them sweet sisters in that haunted place
Where, with child's voices, strong men howl or bleat.

Yet now those men lay stubborn courage by,
Riding dull-eyed and silent in the train
To old men's stools; or sell gay-coloured socks
And listen fearfully for Death; so I
Love the low-laughing girls, who now again
Go daintily, in thin and flowery frocks.

by Edgell Rickword

"The Other Side" By Alec Waugh

Elder brother of Evelyn Waugh; after fighting at Passchendaele, captured near Arras, 1918, so a P.O.W.

There are not any, save the men who died,
Whose minds have probed into the heart of war.
Sometimes we stumble on a secret door
And listening guess what lies the other side.
Sometimes a moment's sudden pain
Flings back the veil that hangs between
Guessing and knowing; then lets it fall again
Before we understand what we have seen.
In and out everywhere,
Distorted in a twisted glass,
Fragmentary visions pass.
We try to fit them one with another,
Like a child putting a puzzle together,
When half the pieces are not there.
Out of a dim obscurity
Certain things stand plain and clear,
Certain things we are forced to see,
Certain things we are forced to hear.
A subaltern dying between the lines,
  Wondering why.
A father with nothing left of life
  But the will to die.

A young girl born for laughter and spring,
Left to her shame and loneliness.
What is one woman more or less
To men who've forgotten everything?

A thin line swinging forward to kill,
  And a man driven mad by the din.
Music-hall songs about "Kaiser Bill"
  And "the march through the streets of Berlin."
Grey-beards prattling round a fire
Of the good the war has done.

Three men rotting upon the wire;
Each of them had a son.
A soldier who once was fresh and clean
Lost to himself in whoring and drink,
Blind to what will be and what has been,

Only aware that he must not think.
In the pulpit a parson preaching lies
Babbling of honour and sacrifice.
Fragments flutter in and out
Christ! what is it all about?

Alec Waugh - Hampstead, March 1917

June 1917, A P Herbert has a go at the General Staff.

"After The Battle"

So they are satisfied with our Brigade,
And it remains to parcel out the bays!
And we shall have the usual Thanks Parade,
The beaming General, and the soapy praise.

You will come up in your capacious car
To find your heroes sulking in the rain,
To tell us how magnificent we are,
And how you hope we'll do the same again.

And we, who knew your old abusive tongue,
Who heard you hector us a week before,
We who have bled to boost you up a rung —
A KCB perhaps, perhaps a Corps —

We who must mourn those spaces in the Mess
And somehow fill those hollows in the heart,
We do not want your Sermon on Success,
Your greasy benisons on Being Smart.

We only want to take our wounds away
To some warm village where the tumult ends,
And drowsing in the sunshine many a day,
Forget our aches, forget that we had friends.

Weary we are of blood and noise and pain;
This was a week we shall not soon forget;
And if, indeed, we have to fight again,
We little wish to think about it yet.

We have done well; we like to hear it said.
Say it, and then, for God's sake, say no more.
Fight, if you must, fresh battles far ahead,
But keep them dark behind your chateau door!

A P Herbert

A A Milne was a well-known writer of humorous verse, essays and plays, before the war. References in this poem to a "Blighty" - he was wounded at the Somme, 7 July 1916 - are biographical. In 1917 he rejoined MI7 - intelligence. He was also a Major in WW2, aged 60, in the Home Guard.

"Gold Braid"

Same old crossing, same old boat,
  Same old dust round Rouen way,
Same old nasty, one-franc note,
  Same old 'Mercy, sivoo play';
Same old scramble up the line.
  Same old 'orse-box, same old stror,
Same old weather, wet or fine,
  Same old blooming War.
        Ho Lor, it isn't a dream,
          It's just as it used to be, every bit;
        Same old whistle and same old bang,
          And me to stay 'ere till I'm 'it.
'Twas up by Loos I got my first;
  I just dropped gently, crawled a yard
And rested sickish, with a thirst -
  The 'eat, I thought, and smoking 'ard...
Then someone offers me a drink,
  What poets call 'the cooling draft',
And seeing 'im I done a think:
  'Blighty' I thinks - and laughed.

I'm not a soldier natural
  No more than most of us to-day;
I runs a business with a pal
  (Meaning the Missis) Fulham way;
Greengrocery — the cabbages
  And fruit and things I take myself,
And she has the daffs and crocuses
  A-smiling on a shelf.

'Blighty' I thinks. The doctor knows;
'E talks of punctured damn-the-things.
It's me for Blighty. Down I goes;
I ain't a singer, but I sings
'Oh, 'oo goes 'ome?' I sort of 'ums
'Oh, 'oo's for dear old England's shores?'
And by-and-by Southampton comes —
'Blighty!' I says and roars.
I s'pose I thort I done my bit;

I s'pose I thort the War would stop;
I saw myself a-getting fit
With Missis at the little shop;
The same like as it used to be,
The same old markets, same old crowd,
The same old marrers, same old me,
But 'er as proud as proud.

* * * * * * * * * * * *

The regiment is where it was,
I'm in the same old ninth platoon;
New faces most, and keen becos
They 'ope the thing is ending soon;
I ain't complaining mind, but still,
When later on some newish bloke
Stops one and laughs, 'A Blighty, Bill',
I'll wonder, 'Where's the joke?'

Same old trenches, same old view,
Same old rats and just as tame,
Same old dug-outs, nothing new,
Same old smell, the very same,
Same old bodies out in front,
Same old strafe from 2 to 4,
Same old scratching, same old 'unt,
Same old bloody War.
Ho Lor, it isn't a dream,
It's just as it used to be, every bit;
Same old whistle and same old bang,
And me out again to be 'it.

A A Milne

Educated at Eton and Oxford, de Stein rose to the rank of Major, serving on the Western Front throughout WWI.

"Envoi" by Edward de Stein

How shall I say goodbye to you, wonderful, terrible days,
If I should live to live and leave 'neath an alien soil
You, my men, who taught me to walk with a smile in the ways
Of the valley of shadows, taught me to know you and love you, and toil
Glad in the glory of fellowship, happy in misery, strong
In the strength that laughs at its weakness, laughs at its sorrows and fears,
Facing the world that was not too kind with a jest and a song?
What can the world hold afterwards worthy of laughter or tears?

AUTHOR INDEX